INVEST WISELY, LIVE FREELY

Your Guide to Financial Clarity, Confidence & Freedom

Vipul Bane

Founder & Financial Coach, Adyanta Financial Services

"Turn Confusion Into Clarity. Turn Money Into Freedom."

BookMyStory®

Invest Wisely, Live Freely
Your Guide to Financial Clarity, Confidence and Freedom
Vipul Bane
Published in 2026

© Published by

BookMyStory®

It's time you tell your story

BookMyStory
Thane, 400615, India
info@bookmystorypublishing.com
www.bookmystorypublishing.com

ISBN: 978-93-49509-52-8 [Paperback / softback]

Foreword

I first met Vipul in April 2020, when he joined LPCC Batch 4. What began as a coach–participant relationship quickly evolved into a bond founded on purpose, authenticity, and a deep human connection. Even then, Vipul stood out—not because of what he knew, but because of who he was. His sincerity, humility, curiosity, and willingness to learn and unlearn made him one of those rare individuals who transform not only their own lives but also the lives of everyone they touch.

Over the years, as I watched Vipul evolve through his journey—from a seasoned financial professional to a purpose-driven financial coach—I realized that his work went far beyond numbers and wealth creation. His approach has always been rooted in clarity, compassion, and contribution. This is beautifully reflected in his guiding principle: **Live More, Give More.** He embodies this philosophy in the way he lives, leads, and serves, and this book is a natural extension of that spirit.

Invest Wisely, Live Freely is not just a book—it is Vipul's mission.

It is the culmination of his 25+ years in the banking and financial world, his interactions with thousands of families, and his own lived experiences of overcoming fear, rebuilding confidence, and eventually achieving freedom. But more importantly, it is his offering to every Indian family seeking clarity amidst financial confusion.

What makes this book extraordinary is its **simplicity.** Vipul has taken concepts that often intimidate people—money mindset, budgeting, asset allocation, retirement planning, financial freedom—and made them accessible, relatable, and practical. He writes the way he coaches: with patience, empathy, and conviction. His conscious choice to replace jargon with everyday language, and to support every idea with real-life stories, is one of the book's greatest strengths.

Vipul's emphasis on **mindset before mechanics,** on behaviour before returns, and on meaning before money sets this book apart. As he rightly states, *"Financial literacy is not just about knowing the math. It's about knowing yourself."* This is financial coaching at its finest—uniting personal awareness with practical action.

I was especially moved by the chapters where Vipul shares his personal journey—his mistakes, fears, setbacks, and inner transformation. The honesty with which he writes makes this book not just informative but inspiring. It reminds every reader that financial freedom is not reserved for the privileged or lucky—it is available to anyone who is willing to take responsibility, build discipline, and align their money with their purpose.

This book is also a reflection of Vipul's gratitude to his father, family, clients, mentors, and spiritual path. It carries the blessings, wisdom, and stories of every person who shaped his journey. And it carries his deep desire to simplify money for 10,000 Indian families and help them live with confidence, dignity, and choice.

As a Purpose Coach, it fills me with pride to witness Vipul living his purpose so powerfully—and gifting the world a book that will change not just finances, but lives.

Dear Reader,

As you begin your journey through these pages, I invite you to absorb not just the knowledge but the intention behind it.

Because this book is not about wealth—it is about **freedom**. And freedom, as Vipul beautifully reminds us, is the true purpose of money.

Your journey to financial clarity, confidence, and freedom starts now.

Nitesh Gawade
Purpose Coach | Speaker
Founder of LPCC Community

About the Author

Vipul Bane (BSc, PGDMS, MHRDM, CPFA, AFP, AFGP) is the Founder and Financial Coach at **Adyanta Financial Services** (Adyanta). With over **25 years of experience,** he has helped individuals and families in India and overseas achieve financial clarity, stability, and freedom.

A seasoned keynote speaker, he has delivered **more than 350 financial workshops, awareness programmes, and conclaves,** simplifying money management in a way that is simple, relatable, and practical for people from all walks of life.

His guiding principle is **'Live More, Give More' — a way of life** that has been part of his life for over a decade.

Live More → through travel, meaningful experiences, and quality time with family and friends, grounded in values of trust, integrity, compassion, and service.

Give More → by supporting causes close to his heart, and generously sharing his time, skills, and knowledge to create positive impact.

His happiness mantra is simple yet profound: **align the 4 Ps — Purpose, Passion, Profession, and Personality.** When they connect, they feel like playing.

Vipul's vision is to **simplify money** and make **financial wisdom accessible** to every literate Indian. His mission is to **empower 10,000 Indian families** to achieve true **financial freedom** and contribute meaningfully to India's journey towards becoming a developed nation.

Over the years, he has received **14 regional and national awards** and touched the lives of more than **1,000 families globally.** Yet, what he values most is **the trust and respect of his clients**, community, and friends — reflected in Adyanta's exceptional **client retention rate of over 99%.**

A lifelong learner and people-focused professional, he continues to inspire through **relatable stories, practical strategies**, and a commitment to helping people turn money into freedom.

You can connect with him on **LinkedIn, Facebook, YouTube,** and **Instagram,** or write to him at **banevipul@gmail.com**

The Story behind This Book

"Money doesn't come with a manual — and this book aims to change that."

There are many well-known books on personal finance, and several have deeply influenced me (refer to Chapter 29), but when I searched for a *simple, practical, India-focused handbook* for families, I couldn't find one.

During my 25+ years in the banking and financial sector, I observed that many people in India, despite earning a high income, are still unable to achieve their dreams, reach their goals, or live freely because they lack clarity, discipline, confidence, or professional guidance.

That's what inspired this book — to provide a clear, **India-focused framework** with actionable steps that build clarity, confidence, and discipline, essential for financial well-being and long-term freedom.

Based on real questions, client interactions, and lived experiences from over 13 years of financial coaching, this book can act as a ready reference for all the busy professionals, families, and freedom seekers who want to make better financial decisions.

Through this book, I want to **share and give** the best practices that I learnt over the years from my mentors and gurus, the knowledge that I gathered from books, certifications, and training programs, and the insights that I gained over the years as a Financial Coach.

Writing this book wasn't just about sharing knowledge or experience — it was about making finance simple. I consciously replaced jargon with simple, everyday language. For terms that may still feel unfamiliar, the glossary at the end will help.

What makes it truly special is the collection of 50+ real-life stories — of people who faced challenges and overcame them, proving the right plan changes everything, and of others who made mistakes but never corrected them. To protect privacy and personal details, a few names have been altered — but the stories and lessons are 100% real.

Lastly, the book gives you deeper insights into **my own journey — from fear to freedom** — where I share my biggest money mistakes, failures, lessons, the mindset that changed my life, and the clear, actionable strategies that helped me realise both time freedom and financial freedom.

Whether you're just starting, juggling multiple goals, or planning your legacy, **this book is your roadmap to financial freedom** — one wise, lively step at a time. If you want a life by design — not by default — start here.

Happy Freedom!! Because the end-goal isn't more money — it's freedom.

Contents

Introduction

From To-Do to Done — A Journey Fueled by Purpose and Passion

Every book has a beginning. This one began long before I put pen to paper — with a dream, a promise, and a purpose.

For years, this book sat on my to-do list and bucket list — competing with chores, cricket matches, client calls, and even idle moments. It finally began as a New Year's resolution on 1 January 2022, and by 23 January, I had announced it on social media with its title, cover design, and an ambitious 90-day launch goal.

But life had other plans, nudging me in ways I couldn't ignore. Six months passed with little progress until I began to visualise the book and sketch an outline. That's when it slowly started taking shape. And once I aligned my passion with my purpose, the book stopped being about a deadline — it became a mission.

That shift kept me grounded, focused, and consistent. It gave me the freedom to enjoy the process, contribute more, and grow through the journey. With content already flowing from my LinkedIn posts, newsletters, presentations, and podcasts, the task became one of compiling, refining, and shaping it into the kind of book I would love to read myself.

Beyond my professional expertise and insights, this book carries a piece of my personal journey. It is a reflection of a path still unfolding, a tribute to those who have walked alongside me, and a torch I hope will light someone else's way. The title — **Invest Wisely, Live Freely** — is more than just a financial mantra; it is a philosophy.

For me, *Invest Wisely* goes far beyond money. It means consciously investing your time, energy, and curiosity to master the art and science of managing it. It means nurturing relationships that uplift you, seeking experiences that bring joy, and committing to personal growth with mentors or coaches who can walk the journey with you.

Living Freely doesn't mean extravagance — it means living life without fear, regret, or stress. It means living on your own terms, where work becomes an option rather than a compulsion. It means having the privilege to make choices without constraints caused by money and having the space to pursue what truly brings joy, purpose, and peace.

No journey is walked alone, and this one certainly wasn't.

This book is dedicated first and foremost to my father, **the late Shri Ravindra Harishchandra Bane** — the man who believed in me unwaveringly, stood by me always, and even beyond this physical world continues to guide and inspire me with his resilience, values, and spirit. Dad, this one is for you.

To all our **esteemed clients** — more than clients, many of you are friends, extended family, and fellow travellers on this journey. Your stories, trust, wins (and even fears), feedback, and words of encouragement are the true heartbeat of this book. You have shown me what financial freedom means across different walks of life.

To my wife, **Harshal Bane** — what can I say? You have been my rock, my voice of reason, and my biggest cheerleader. Without your unwavering belief, I would never have dared to step into entrepreneurship, let alone write a book about financial freedom. You held the fort, held my hand, and sometimes even held back your worries so I could pursue my dreams. Thank you for being my silent strength and my loudest supporter.

To my son, **Jairaj** — your excitement for this book was contagious. Your questions, curiosity, and constant "Papa, when will the book launch?" became the most innocent yet powerful deadline reminder I could ever ask for. I hope that one day, when you read this, you see not just your father's journey, but also your part in shaping it.

I extend my deepest gratitude to my revered Spiritual Guru, **Sri Sri Ravi Shankar,** whose blessings have been a guiding light on my path, and to the entire Art of Living family, whose wisdom and support have been pivotal in my personal transformation.

My heartfelt gratitude to **Mr Nitesh Gawade - Purpose Coach,** whose powerful foreword and purpose-driven perspective adds immense meaning to this book.

A heartfelt thank you to my team at Adyanta Financial Services, especially **Shalini Kulshrestha**, who took my phone calls at odd hours and even on holidays, read my emails and WhatsApp messages, sifted through sketches and scattered client stories, and helped turn them into something coherent and meaningful.

To my sister, **Darshana Padghane** — your unwavering faith and strength have been my constant anchor.

To the entire Prudent family, ably led by **Mr Sanjay Shah (MD)** and **Mr Shirish Patel (CEO)**, my sincere gratitude for your steadfast support and belief that made this journey possible.

The inspiring LPCC community — thank you for reminding me to live and write with intention and purpose.

And to my **tribe — friends, colleagues, and well-wishers** — your candid feedback, kind words, and timely nudges breathed life into these pages.

Special thanks to **Mr. Sanjay Shah** and **Dr. Radhakrishnan Pillai** for reviewing this book — your thoughtful insights have added depth and meaning to this work.

Each of you, in your own way, has left an imprint on this book. Every word carries a bit of your energy, and for that, I am deeply grateful.

This book goes beyond personal finance — it is a practical handbook, a guiding torch, and a tribute to building both wealth and a fulfilling life.

So, whether you are just starting, feeling stuck, or searching for clarity amidst financial chaos, know this:

- You are not alone.
- It is never too late.

And smart money moves aren't about magic — they are about the right mindset, method, and momentum.

Turn the page — your journey to financial freedom might just begin here.

In Loving Memory Of

Late Shri Ravindra Harishchandra Bane

"A man whose integrity and generosity remain my greatest inheritance."

Wealth with Purpose

As you step ahead to chart your way,
Let purpose be the light of each day.
For money's a vessel, a passage, a friend—
A means to the journey, but never the end.

True riches are measured in trust that you sow,
In kindness extended, in love that will grow.
The lives that you brighten, the hope you renew,
These treasures are timeless and shine within you.

My father once showed me, with wisdom so deep,
That integrity's wealth is the one we must keep.
In giving, in caring, in standing up true,
He gifted a compass to help me pull through.

His values still whisper, they steady, they guide,
A legacy etched, like the stars in the sky.
And through these pages, I hope they'll impart,
A wealth for your soul, and a light for your heart.

"The richest legacy is not money left behind, but values lived every day."

Your Wheel of Life — Where Are You Standing Today?

Before we dive into strategies and stories, take a moment to reflect on your life as it stands right now. Let's begin with a simple yet powerful exercise:

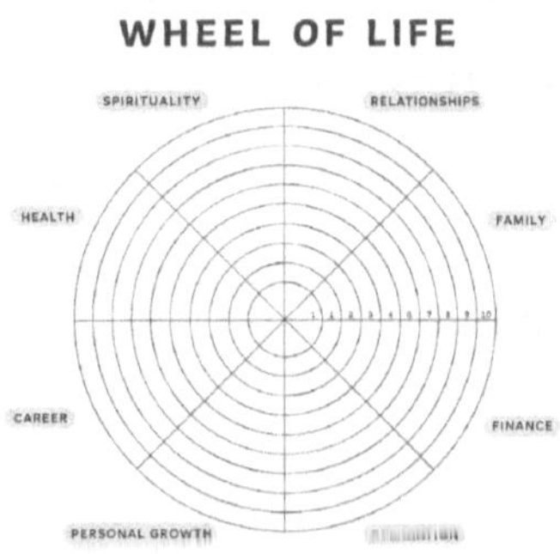

1. Rate yourself in each area of life from 1 (low) to 10 (high) in the above diagram.
2. Colour each of the sections and draw a line using a pencil to connect the points as shown below:

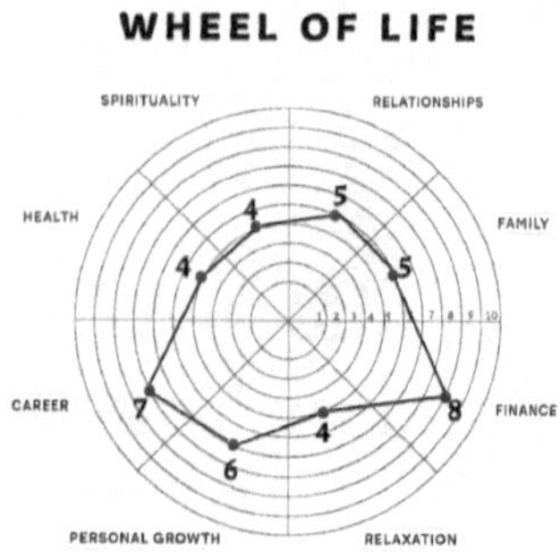

"Wheel of Life—reference diagram"

3. Look at the shape you have drawn: Is your wheel balanced enough to roll smoothly?
4. Now, sketch your ideal "Dream Life" in the wheel of life given below to show where you want to be.

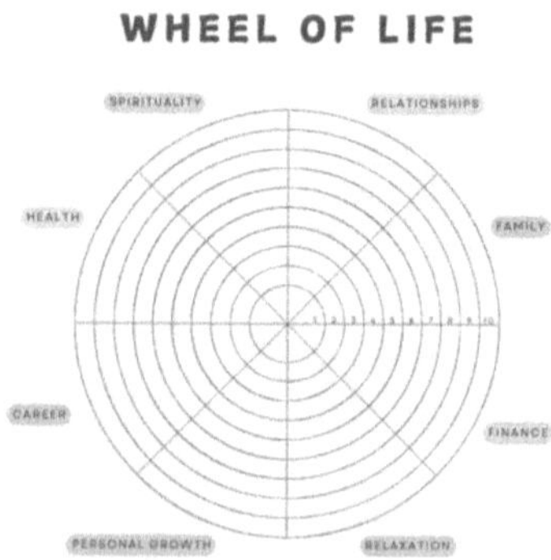

"A well-balanced life creates a wealth-secured future."

Disclaimer

Read Before You Act

This book is designed to educate, empower, and inspire you on your financial journey. The concepts, stories, examples, and illustrations shared are intended solely for educational purposes.

By no means do they constitute financial advice, product endorsements, or personalised recommendations.

Every reader's financial situation, goals, and risk profile are unique. It is strongly advised that you consult a qualified financial professional before making any investment, tax, or financial decisions.

The author and publisher assume no responsibility or liability for any loss, damage, or adverse consequences, direct or indirect, that may result from the application of the ideas presented in this book.

Important Regulatory Note:

- Mutual Fund investments are subject to market risks. Please read all scheme-related documents carefully before investing.
- Past performance is not indicative of future results.
- Tax laws, investment regulations, and financial products may change over time — always seek the most updated information.

This book is about clarity, not certainty. Use it as a guide to ask the right questions, build awareness, and take action with confidence — but always with informed, professional advice tailored to your own circumstances.

The Six Pillars of Financial Freedom

Your journey through this book rests on six interconnected pillars. Each pillar supports the next, creating a complete path toward clarity, confidence, and freedom.

Pillar 1: Mindset & Awareness

Clear limiting beliefs, strengthen financial literacy, and build the right money mindset.

Pillar 2: Protect & Prepare

Secure your foundation with budgeting, insurance, family conversations, women's wealth, and tax planning.

Pillar 3: Grow & Allocate

Build lasting wealth through risk profiling, asset allocation, mutual funds, goal planning, and disciplined reviews.

Pillar 4: Retire & Pass On

Plan for a worry-free retirement, give while alive, and leave a meaningful legacy.

Pillar 5: Adapt & Evolve

Prepare the next generation, embrace new investment trends, and grow with the guidance of a coach.

Pillar 6: Reflect & Apply

Learn from pitfalls, apply lessons, use action plans and mantras, and discover freedom beyond money.

Together, these six pillars and the 32 chapters form your complete roadmap to Financial Freedom.

PILLAR 1

MINDSET & AWARENESS

Wealth begins in the mind. Clear limiting beliefs, strengthen awareness, and build a money mindset that sets the tone for everything that follows.

Chapter 1

The Foundation of Wealth— Financial Literacy Made Simple

"An investment in knowledge pays the best interest."

— Benjamin Franklin

Imagine you are 40 years old. Life's major financial milestones are taken care of — your retirement planning is on track, your children's education is secured, and your family's protection needs are covered.

You even have a surplus of **₹2 Crore (Cr).**

Then comes the dream moment: you find a home worth ₹2 Cr.

Your instinct says:
"I have the money. Let me buy it outright."

But pause for a moment.
That instinct, although comforting, might not be the smartest financial decision.

Being debt-free sounds ideal, but it is not always financially optimal.

So, let us explore the choices you actually have.

- **Option 1: Loan + Invest Surplus**

Suppose you pay **₹20 lakh** as a down payment, take a **20-year home loan at 8%**, and invest the remaining **₹1.80 Cr** at an expected **8% compound annual growth rate (CAGR).**

Monthly EMI = ₹1.5 lakh

Total interest paid over 20 years = ₹1.81 Cr (assuming no prepayment and a stable rate)

Value of ₹1.80 Cr at 8% CAGR after 20 years = ₹8.39 Cr

At the end of 20 years:

Value of the house (8% CAGR) = ₹9.32 Cr

Value of investments = ₹8.39 Cr

Total Wealth = ₹17.71 Cr

It looks straightforward, doesn't it?

A disciplined investor borrows wisely and allows their money to grow — a decision that appears mathematically superior.

- **Option 2: Buy Outright + SIP Discipline**

Now consider another approach.

You buy the home outright using your ₹2 Cr surplus. Since there is no EMI burden, you invest the same **₹1.5 lakh per month** through a **Systematic Investment Plan (SIP)** in mutual funds, expecting a **12% CAGR** over 20 years.

At the end of 20 years:

Value of SIP (12% CAGR) = ₹14.83 Cr

Value of the house = ₹9.32 Cr

Total Wealth = ₹24.15 Cr

Suddenly, this appears to be the winning strategy.

Reality Check:

On paper, yes — Option 2 creates more wealth.

But here is the catch, and this is where most people lose money:

In real life, very few individuals invest **₹1.5 lakh every single month** for 20 years without fail.

What typically happens?

People invest **half** (say, ₹75,000 per month), while the remaining ₹75,000 quietly slips into lifestyle upgrades — a bigger car, more holidays, or occasional indulgences that feel justified with a higher income.

If you invest only ₹75,000 per month:

Value after 20 years = ₹7.42 Cr

Total wealth = ₹7.42 Cr + ₹9.32 Cr (house)

Total = ₹16.74 Cr

This is **lower than Option 1.**

One small behavioural slip creates a massive long-term difference.

Lesson: Whether you take a home loan or buy outright matters far less than your **investment discipline.**

The wise investor invests with discipline, clarity, and confidence to create lasting wealth and achieve true freedom.

The Real Lesson:

Financial literacy is not only about understanding numbers.
It is about understanding **yourself.**

Knowledge tells you which option creates more wealth.
Behaviour decides whether you will actually follow through.

The difference between the wealthy and the not-so-wealthy often comes down to:

Clarity + Discipline

Vs.

Emotion + Distraction

This book is not just about strategies, tools, and formulas.
It is about the mindset and behaviours that determine whether you win or lose with money.

The Silent Gap

Many people assume that a secure job, a high income, a profitable business, or an impressive academic degree guarantees financial success.

Reality tells a different story.

India remains one of the world's fastest-growing economies — yet financial literacy levels are surprisingly low. Even educated professionals, doctors, engineers, business owners, and senior IT employees struggle with essentials like emergency funds, sensible borrowing, or retirement planning.

A recent SEBI investor survey revealed that while **63% of Indian households are aware of at least one market product** (such as mutual funds, ETFs, shares, F&O, REITs, bonds, or AIFs), *awareness alone is not enough.*

True financial success requires:
Understanding → Alignment → Action

As the saying goes:
"It is not your income, but your financial literacy and behaviour that determine your wealth."

Why Most People Lose Money

- They do not lose money because markets are bad — but because their habits are.
- They confuse "earning well" with "managing money well."
- They fall into traps: credit card rollovers, "no-cost" EMIs, and unsuitable insurance products.
- They lack awareness of simple, powerful tools like SIPs, term insurance, emergency funds, and asset allocation.

- They lose wealth through delayed decisions or incorrect choices.

This chapter aims to fix those gaps before you begin chasing big financial goals.

Client Story: The High Earner, Low Saver

Ravi, a 38-year-old senior IT manager in Pune, earned nearly **₹40 lakh per year.** On paper, he appeared financially secure. But when his father faced a medical emergency, Ravi realised that:

He had no emergency fund,

no adequate health insurance, and

Loans consume 60% of his salary.

Despite earning well, he was **"asset-poor."**

Only after building his basics — term insurance, medical cover, and regular SIPs — did his finances finally stabilise.

"Income without literacy is like water in a leaking bucket."

The Five Pillars of Financial Literacy

1. **Earning** - Income is the starting point, not the end goal.
2. **Spending** - Budget wisely; Avoid lifestyle creep as your income increases
3. **Saving** - Save first, spend later. Treat savings like a mandatory bill.

4. **Investing** – Put your money to work. Compounding outperforms Idle cash.

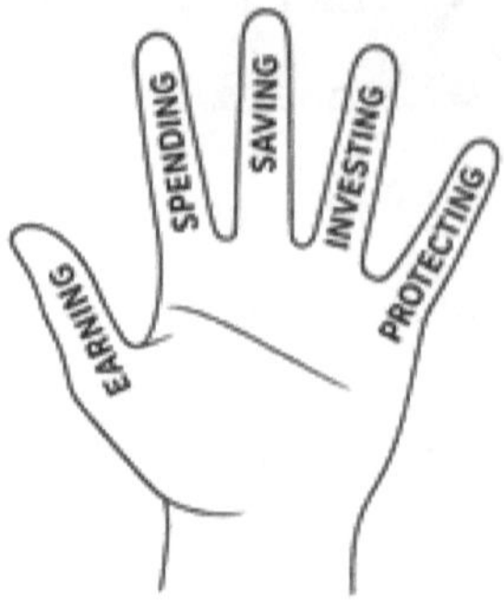

5. **Protecting** – Safeguard your wealth with insurance, emergency funds, and controlled debt.

Client Story: The Homemaker Who Won

Meera, a 45-year-old homemaker in Thane, handled only household responsibilities while her husband managed all financial matters. After attending a financial awareness session, she started a modest **₹3,000 monthly SIP** and learnt the difference between **good debt and bad debt.**

When her husband unexpectedly lost his job for six months, Meera's small but disciplined savings became the family's survival fund.

That experience empowered her to become actively involved in the family's finances.

"Financial literacy is not about how much you earn, but how much control you have."

Financial Literacy Questionnaire: Test Yourself

Answer quick Yes/No questions—just 2 minutes to gauge your financial literacy.

Your scorecard: Yes =1 point, No = 0; **Check your score and know where you stand**

1. Do you know how much you save (as % of income) each month?
2. Do you have an emergency fund covering at least 6 months of expenses?
3. Do you understand the difference between term insurance and endowment insurance?
4. Do you know how much money you will approximately need for retirement?
5. Do you invest regularly (e.g., SIPs) instead of waiting for the "right time"?
6. Do you review your portfolio and financial goals at least once a year?
7. Do you avoid debt traps like credit card rollovers or "no-cost" EMIs?
8. Do you discuss financial matters openly with your spouse/family?
9. Do you know your current net worth (assets – liabilities)?
10. Do you have a written financial plan or roadmap?

Scoring:

- 8–10 points: **Strong foundation** — *you're on the right track.*

- 5–7 points: **Average** — *risk of gaps, needs fixing.*
- 0–4 points: **Weak literacy** — *urgent action needed before it's too late.*

"The more you simplify money, the more it works for you."

Key Takeaways:

- Financial literacy is not optional; it is essential for survival in modern life.
- Wealth is built on five pillars: **earn, spend, save, invest, protect.**
- The questionnaire offers a mirror to help you understand where you currently stand.
- If your literacy is weak or average, this book will help you strengthen it.
- If you already have a strong foundation, this book will help transform knowledge into action.

Now that you have understood the basics, let us move deeper.

Literacy is about knowledge, but wealth also depends on how your mind and emotions behave with money.

In the next chapters, we will uncover the beliefs, mindset, and behavioural biases that silently shape your financial destiny.

Chapter 2

Limiting Money Beliefs and Mind Blocks—How to Clear Those?

"Whether you think you can or think you can't, you're right."

— Henry Ford

Money problems rarely begin when a bank balance turns red. They usually begin long before that — in the mind.

From childhood, we absorb stories about money: whispered warnings from parents, observations from relatives, cultural messages, and the lessons embedded in our own experiences. Some of these stories uplift us. Many quietly limit us.

These limiting beliefs become invisible chains.

You may work hard, earn well, and still feel stuck, stressed, or unable to build lasting wealth.

To change your financial life, you must first change your relationship with money.

Do You Love Money?

Do you love money — honestly, consciously, and without guilt?
Or do you simply chase it, fear it, criticise it, or hide from it?
Many of us grow up hearing:

- "Money is the root of all evil."
- "Rich people are selfish."
- "Spirituality and wealth don't go together."

Because of such conditioning, people often love money secretly, but hate it publicly. They crave wealth but feel guilty for wanting it.

Here is the quieter truth:

Money is like energy.

It can flow, stagnate, grow, or drain — depending on the intention behind it.

- If you hoard money with fear, it becomes stagnant.
- If you circulate money with gratitude, it multiplies.
- If you see money as power, it can make you restless.
- If you see money as a purpose, it can bring peace.

Loving money is not wrong. **Attachment is.**

True love for money is like a gardener's love for rain — not to possess it, but to use it wisely to nourish life.

When you earn with integrity, spend with awareness, save with discipline, and give with joy,

You honour money — and money honours you back.

Self-Reflection:

"Do I see money as a master, a mirror, or a medium of meaning?"

What's Your Relationship with Money?

If money were a person, how would you describe your relationship with it?

Money is more than a medium of exchange. It reflects your beliefs, emotions, and mindset.

For some, money is a friend that provides freedom.
For others, it is a foe that causes stress and sleepless nights.
For many, it is a silent partner — present but rarely understood.

Over the past 25 years, I have observed that people generally fall into three financial behaviour patterns:

1. **Money Disorder** → Overspending, avoidance, hoarding, impulsive buying, or chasing money at the cost of peace. This feels like being trapped in a toxic cycle.

2. **Money Anxiety** → The constant fear of "never having enough", even when financially stable. This shows up as guilt about spending or stress about the future.

3. **Money Magnet** → A healthy, abundant mindset where money flows with clarity, discipline, and purpose. This mindset attracts opportunities not through luck, but through trust, gratitude, and wise action.

Your goal is to move from disorder and anxiety to becoming a money magnet — where money becomes a supportive partner, not a demanding master.

Self-Reflection Quiz:

1. **When you think about money, what's your first feeling?**

    a. Stress → Disorder

    b. Worry → Anxiety

    c. Clarity → Magnet

2. **How do you handle unexpected expenses?**

    a. Panic → Disorder

    b. Manage with worry → Anxiety

    c. Adjust calmly → Magnet

3. **Do you track your income and spending?**

    a. Rarely → Disorder

    b. Sometimes, with guilt → Anxiety

    c. Consistently, with confidence → Magnet

Mostly a's → You need healing and structure.

Mostly b's → Build confidence through planning.

Mostly c's → You're on the path of a money magnet.

"Money is neither good nor bad— it simply reflects the mindset you bring to it."

How to Become a Money Magnet

Attract Wealth with Intention, Emotion, and Energy.

Wealth is not chased — it is attracted.

Your thoughts, emotions, and actions become the magnet that draws opportunities towards you.

Here are three powerful techniques used by financially grounded people:

1. **Positive Affirmations – Rewire Your Beliefs**

Your words shape your inner world. Begin each morning with empowering statements such as:

- "Money flows to me with ease and purpose."
- "I am open to receiving prosperity."
- "I make wise, confident financial decisions."

Repeated daily, affirmations train the subconscious mind to expect abundance instead of scarcity.

2. **Power of Visualisation – See It, Feel It, Live It**

(Visualisation = mentally imagining a desired financial outcome)

Close your eyes and imagine your ideal financial life — your home, your freedom, the choices, the peace. Visualisation activates the same neural pathways as experience, preparing your mind to recognise and act on opportunities.

Emotion fuels manifestation — feel the joy and gratitude of already having it.

3. Releasing Negative Patterns – Let Go and Reset

Many people carry limiting beliefs such as:

"Money is hard to earn," "I'm not good with money," "Wealthy people are greedy."

Write these beliefs on paper, read them aloud, and then safely tear or burn the paper.

This symbolic act signals to the subconscious mind that it is time to release old patterns and embrace new ones.

"Money flows towards those who respect it, manage it, and align with its rhythm."

Common Limiting Money Beliefs

1. *"I'm just not good with money."* — Becomes a self-fulfilling prophecy and stops you from learning.
2. *"Rich people are selfish."* — Creates internal conflict — you want wealth but do not want to become "one of them."
3. *"I don't deserve to be wealthy."* — Often rooted in low self-

worth, this belief restricts earning potential.

4. *"Early retirement is only for the lucky or privileged."* — You close the door before even checking what is possible.
5. *"Spending on myself is selfish."* — Delays joy and self-care, even when affordable.

Three Types of Money Mind Blocks

The Money Mind blocks can be classified into 3 main categories:

- **Fear-based Blocks** → Fear of Loss, Scarcity mindset, Risk Aversion.
- **Ego/Comparison Blocks** → Overconfidence, Status-driven spending, Peer Pressure.
- **Inaction Blocks** → Procrastination, Dependency, Short-term thinking.

Emotions Over Logic

Equity Markets run on two primary emotions—**fear and greed.**

Most investors succumb to these cycles.

- When markets rise, greed whispers: *"Buy more, you'll miss out!"*
- When markets fall, fear screams: *"Sell now before it's too late!"*

In such moments, logic is pushed aside, and emotions take over — leading to poor decisions.

Client Story: Panic vs Patience — During the 2020 Market Crash

In March 2020, when COVID-19 struck, Indian equity markets fell by nearly **40% within weeks.**

Abhishek, a new investor, panicked and exited all his equity mutual funds at a loss.

His fear convinced him that markets would collapse further.

Meanwhile, other clients who remained patient — or even invested more — saw their portfolios recover and touch new highs within a year.

Lesson: Emotion-driven investors lose money, while disciplined, logic-driven investors create long-term wealth.

"Money mistakes rarely come from lack of intelligence. They come from letting emotions override discipline."

The 5 Money Myths That Hold People Back

1. *'I'll save whatever is left after spending'* → No, save first, spend later.
2. *'EMIs are manageable'* → They may be today, but they

restrict future cash flow.

3. *'Insurance is a waste if nothing happens'* → Insurance is a parachute, not a lottery.
4. *'I'll start investing once I earn more'* → You won't. You must start now.
5. *'I don't need a financial advisor'* → Influencers can't replace a personalised financial strategy.

"Financial success is not a hard science. It's a soft skill, where how you behave is more important than what you know."— **Morgan Housel** in the book -The Psychology of Money.

Where Limiting Beliefs, Myths, or Mind Blocks Come From

No one is born with limiting beliefs, myths, or money blocks — they're shaped over time by our experiences, environment, and influences. They may come from:

- **Family Conditioning** — People like us never become rich."
- **Cultural Narratives** — Glorifying struggle, mistrusting success.
- **Past Failures** — losses, betrayals, bad investments.
- **Peer Influence** — Friends normalising debt or overspending.
- **Fixed Mindset**— believing abilities cannot be improved.

Story: The Price of Financial Fear

Dr Rajesh, a brilliant professor, lived a disciplined life — teaching, writing, and selling insurance part-time. He saved more than 40% of his income, mostly in fixed deposits.

But past scars controlled him:

A failed business, a partner's betrayal, and a significant stock market loss.

These experiences shaped his beliefs:

"I'm bad with money. I can never retire early."

Though intelligent, he avoided equity investments and ignored opportunities.

Fear guided his decisions more than logic.

In the end, fear cost him more than money — it cost him peace, growth, and freedom.

"Limiting beliefs don't just shrink your returns — they shrink your life."

The Cost of Holding On

Limiting Money beliefs, Mind Blocks, and Myths don't just affect your thoughts—they affect your actions:

- Avoiding profitable opportunities.
- Remaining in low-paying jobs.
- Undervaluing your skills.
- Living in survival mode.
- Staying stuck in your comfort zone.

As a result, many people never achieve financial independence — not due to lack of income, but due to self-imposed mental barriers.

Client Story: Shift the Story, Shape the Future

Minakshi earned well but avoided investing. Her belief: **"Markets are gambling."**

We later discovered her father had lost money decades ago in a chit fund — a completely different product from today's regulated investment options.

We started small with short-term debt funds, then gradually introduced equity.

Today, Minakshi has a diversified portfolio and is on track to retire **seven years earlier.**

The breakthrough wasn't an investment product — it was the story she believed.

"Change your beliefs, and you change your financial destiny."

From Limiting Beliefs to Empowering Beliefs

Your beliefs form your Money Blueprint. Once you break your limiting money beliefs, you free yourself to make bold, smart, and confident decisions.

Limiting Belief	Why It Holds You Back	Empowering Belief
Money is the root of evil.	Creates guilt and repels wealth.	Money is a tool—its impact depends on how I use it.
I'm not good with money.	Stops learning and growth.	I can learn money skills and improve daily.
Rich people are selfish.	Creates inner conflict.	Wealth allows me to help others.
I don't deserve wealth.	Diminishes self-worth.	I deserve financial freedom.
I'll never retire early.	Blocks action and planning.	With the right plan, I can retire on my terms.
Spending on myself is selfish.	Delays joy and well-being.	Investing in myself increases my capacity to contribute.

How to Clear Limiting Money Beliefs

1. **Identify Them** — Write down the money messages you heard growing up and the phrases you repeat to yourself.

2. **Challenge Them with Facts** — Ask Is this always true? Who taught me this? Are there examples that prove it wrong?

3. **Replace with Empowering Beliefs** — 'Money is scarce' → 'Money is a tool, and I can learn to manage well.'

4. **Take Small, Positive Actions** — Beliefs change faster when you act against them.

5. **Surround Yourself with the Right Influence** — Be with people who have a healthy, abundant relationship with money.

Chapter 3

Mind Over Money – Building the Right Financial Mindset

"The mind is everything. What you think you become."

— Buddha

Most people assume that financial success comes from earning a high income or making clever investments. Yet the deeper truth is this:

"Your mindset shapes your money decisions far more than any stock market does."

Beliefs and mindset are connected, but they are not the same.

Beliefs are the stories we tell ourselves about money, success, or life.

Mindset is the larger framework that determines whether we believe our abilities, habits, and outcomes can change.

If mindset is the soil, then beliefs are the plants that grow from it.

Nurture the soil, and the plants flourish.

Fixed vs. Growth Mindset

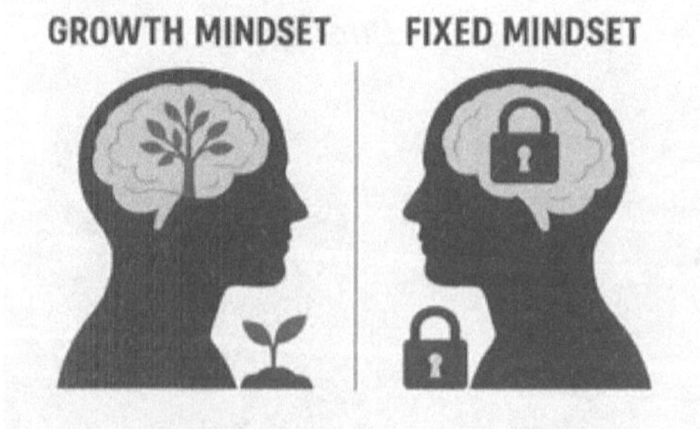

The way we think about money strongly influences the financial results we achieve. A fixed mindset creates limiting beliefs and avoidance behaviour; a growth mindset builds confidence, resilience, and progress.

Psychologist Carol Dweck's work on fixed and growth mindsets applies as much to money as it does to learning and personal development.

- **Fixed Mindset:** A fixed mindset assumes that personal qualities — such as intelligence, discipline, or financial ability — are unchangeable. This often leads to avoiding challenges, fearing mistakes, and giving up easily.
- **Growth Mindset:** A growth mindset believes that abilities can be developed through learning, discipline, and consistent effort. This fosters curiosity, resilience, and a willingness to try again.

This shift — from limitation to possibility — can profoundly transform your financial journey.

Client Story: The Engineer Who Transformed His Finances

Kishor Choudhari, a software engineer, once told me, *"I'll never invest in equity markets as they are risky, and I do not want to lose money."* This was a classic Fixed Mindset—avoiding financial growth out of fear.

We began with small, manageable steps. Rather than chasing high returns, Kishor started a modest **Systematic Investment Plan (SIP)** of ₹30,000 in 2018. As he witnessed gradual progress, curiosity replaced fear. With guidance, he increased his investments.

Seven years later, his portfolio is already ₹1 crore + (as of 20th Nov. 2025), with a **Compound Annual Growth Rate (CAGR)** of over 18%. More importantly, his mindset has transformed.

He now says, ***"Investing is a skill. The more I learn, the better I become."***

His journey moved from fear to curiosity, from avoidance to confidence — a true shift into a growth mindset.

"Wealth begins not in your bank account, but in your mindset."

S.No.	Fixed Mindset	Growth Mindset
1	"I'm bad with money."	"I can learn to manage money better."
2	"Investing is risky, so I'll avoid it."	"Investing is a skill I can build over time."
3	"Wealth is only for the lucky or privileged."	"Wealth can be created with discipline & planning."
4	"I can't change my financial situation."	"Every small step improves my financial future."
5	"One mistake means I'm a failure."	"Mistakes are lessons that make me wiser."

Scarcity vs. Abundance Mindset

While the growth mindset helps us improve our skills, another powerful layer influences our money behaviour: whether we think in terms of scarcity or abundance.

- **Scarcity Mindset:** A scarcity mindset views life through a lens of limitation. It assumes resources are finite and insufficient. This fuels worry, competition, comparison, and a constant fear of missing out.

People with a scarcity mindset:

- Focus on what they lack rather than what is possible
- Hoard money instead of investing
- View others' success as a threat

- **Abundance Mindset:** An abundance mindset sees opportunities rather than limitations. It believes there is enough for everyone, and wealth can grow through creativity, collaboration, and value creation.

People with an abundance mindset:

- Share, contribute, and invest for growth
- Celebrate others' success
- Make decisions from confidence rather than fear

"People with an abundance mindset live with a freedom rooted in trust, possibility, and self-belief."

Client Story: Neha's Mindset Makeover

Neha, a 36-year-old IT professional from Pune, felt trapped in debt and self-doubt. Her **CIBIL score** had dropped to 620 after repeated **Equated Monthly Instalment (EMI)** defaults. Anxiety, guilt, and scarcity thinking consumed her.

Through conscious budgeting, gratitude journaling, and the habit of giving, she gradually shifted into an abundance mindset.

Within three years:

- She cleared all her debt
- Accumulated over ₹5.4 lakh in investments
- Planned her dream holiday
- Improved her CIBIL score to 755
- Regained confidence, clarity, and emotional balance

Her true transformation was not just financial — it was psychological.

"Money follows effort; wealth follows mindset."

Pause and Reflect

Before moving forward, take a moment to reflect on your current money mindset.

1. **When you hear the word "wealth," what does it mean to you?**

    a) Having lots of money

    b) Being financially stable and comfortable

    c) Living freely, with choices and fulfilment

2. **How do you react to a financial setback (job loss, market correction)?**

    a) Panic or freeze

    b) Adjust lifestyle and wait it out

    c) See it as an opportunity to reset and grow

3. **Which statement feels closest to your belief?**

    a) "Money is scarce — I must hold on tightly."

    b) "Money matters, but it isn't everything."

    c) "Money is energy — it flows when managed with purpose."

Mostly a's → Scarcity Mindset: Tends to block opportunities, driven by fear.

Mostly b's → Transitional Mindset: Practical, but can grow further.

Mostly c's → Abundance Mindset: Sees money as a tool for growth, giving, and freedom.

"Mindset is a habit—like a muscle, it strengthens with practice and awareness."

Redefining Happiness for a Healthy Money Mindset

"Happiness is the gentle unfolding of who we are becoming— a continuous evolution towards our highest, truest self."

In the pursuit of success, we often chase numbers, milestones, and possessions. Yet genuine wealth lies in life's simplest joys.

Happiness is not an external destination. It is a quiet, inner movement — a becoming.

In 2020, during an assignment with Visual Facilitation Coach Piyush Modi, I created a doodle titled **"What Makes Me Happy"**. That simple exercise reminded me that true happiness is rooted in the small, meaningful moments that nourish the spirit.

Wealth without joy is incomplete. Joy without purpose is short-lived.

True abundance begins when money aligns with meaning.

True abundance flows when money aligns with meaning — when our financial goals serve our emotional well-being, not the other way around. Your own sketch may awaken the quiet joys and dreams you've forgotten to celebrate.

"True wealth begins with knowing what truly makes you happy."

Your Turn: Create Your 'Happiness Sketch'

Pause and reflect on what genuinely makes you happy — beyond titles, possessions, or financial milestones.

Create your own simple doodle of **2 to 6 things** that bring you joy:

For *instance:* A cup of chai with family, a sunset walk, music, laughter, gardening, and helping someone in need.

When you acknowledge these simple joys, you shift from scarcity to abundance — from chasing wealth to living a meaningful life.

What is Financial Freedom—And Why Does It Matter So Much?

Financial Freedom isn't about yachts, luxury watches, or never working again.

It's about having choices.

- The freedom from paycheque-to-paycheque stress
- The ability to work because you want to, not because you must

- The comfort of knowing your future is secure
- The ease of letting your money work for you

Most people do not lack money. They lack a roadmap.

Our structured 7-Step Financial Freedom Framework at Adyanta Financials has guided hundreds toward financial freedom across incomes and life stages. (Details in Chapter 25)

Billionaire Mindset

A billionaire mindset isn't about wealth alone — it is about how you think, act, and approach opportunities.

Not every billionaire is alike, but their mindset patterns often are:

Core Traits of this Mindset:

- **Abundance Thinking** — wealth can always be created
- **Long-Term Vision** — focus on impact rather than immediate gain
- **Calculated Risk-Taking**— pursuing asymmetric opportunities
- **Obsessive Learning**— continuously upgrading knowledge
- **Problem-Solving Orientation**— treating problems as opportunities
- **Leverage Mindset**— using systems, people, and capital wisely.
- **Resilience & Adaptability**— recovering quickly from setbacks

- **Networking & Relationships**—They understand that big opportunities often come through people, not just ideas.
- **Focus on Value Creation**— wealth follows value
- **Discipline & Habits** — mastering time, energy, and space

"A billionaire mindset is about vision, value creation, leverage, and resilience — not simple money."

Key Learnings:

1. **Think Long-Term & Set Clear Goals**— Wealth isn't built overnight. Define what financial freedom means to you and align your short-, medium-, and long-term goals with a clear purpose and time frame.
2. **Prioritise Saving & Investing** — Pay yourself before you spend. Make saving and investing a non-negotiable habit rather than an afterthought.
3. **Embrace Discipline & Delayed Gratification**— Resist impulsive spending and avoid emotional decisions. Staying disciplined during market swings or temptations today leads to bigger rewards tomorrow.
4. **Focus on Growth, Not Comparison**— Keep learning, upskilling, and taking smart risks outside your comfort zone. Don't measure your progress against others—your journey is unique.

5. **Adopt an Abundance Mindset & Give Back**— Believe that wealth flows when managed with purpose. Practice gratitude and giving—when you create value for others, abundance multiplies.

"The biggest upgrade you can give your finances is upgrading your mindset.

Chapter 4

Behavioural Aspects of Money —Biases and Influences

"The investor's chief problem — and even his worst enemy — is likely to be himself."

— Benjamin Graham

"Money is rarely about the number; It's mostly about behaviour."

Most financial decisions have little to do with spreadsheets, formulas, or calculators. They are shaped by our emotions, habits, upbringing, environment, and the stories we tell ourselves about money. Human brains, although powerful, are not naturally wired for flawless rational thinking. Fear, greed, pride, doubt, and social pressure often dictate our choices long before logic gets a chance to speak.

From impulsive spending to chasing quick returns, it is behaviour—not income or intelligence—that ultimately determines financial outcomes.

In this chapter, we explore the hidden behavioural forces that influence how we earn, spend, save, and invest.

Cognitive Biases – The Invisible Blind Spots

Cognitive biases are mental shortcuts we use to simplify decisions. They can be helpful in daily life, but when it comes to money, they often lead us astray.

- **Overconfidence Bias:** Believing we can consistently 'beat the market' or identify the next *multi-bagger* (a stock expected to multiply in value several times). Overconfidence leads to excessive trading, speculative bets, and ignoring risks.

- **Anchoring Bias:** Fixating on the first piece of information we receive—for example, clinging to a stock's previous high price and refusing to reassess expectations even when conditions have changed.
- **Loss Aversion:** The pain of losing ₹100 feels far greater than the pleasure of gaining ₹100. This makes people:
    - Sell winning investments too early
    - Hold losing investments for too long
    - Avoid opportunities because "what if I'm wrong?"
- **Recency Bias:** Assuming that recent trends will continue indefinitely. For example, heavily investing in technology shares simply because they rallied recently.

Awareness does not eliminate biases, but it helps us pause, reflect, and make better decisions.

Emotional Biases – When Feelings Take Over

Money is deeply emotional. Pride, guilt, fear, excitement, and comparison all influence how we behave. Most people lose money not due to lack of knowledge, but because they fail to manage their emotions.

- **Fear & Greed:**

  Fear triggers panic selling during market dips.

  Greed pushes people to buy aggressively during bull markets.

These emotional extremes can destroy long-term wealth.

- **Endowment Effect:** We tend to overvalue what we own simply because we chose it.

  Example: Refusing to sell a poorly performing stock because "it must recover—I picked it!"

- **Regret Aversion:** Avoiding decisions to avoid the possibility of being wrong. Ironically, indecision often leads to missed opportunities.

- **FOMO (Fear of Missing Out):** Whether it's chasing hot stocks, crypto rallies, or festive 'last day' offers, the FOMO (modern money trap) drives people to act against logic and their own goals.

"Emotions are natural, but systems like SIPs, asset allocation, and financial plans act as guardrails to keep our feelings from wrecking our wealth."

Client Story— When emotions rule, wealth suffers

Jigar Mehta, a Chartered Accountant from a town near Mumbai, and his wife, Jigna, had been building wealth steadily through goal-based SIPs. Their portfolio was performing exceptionally well.

Then a sudden windfall arrived.

Driven by FOMO and peer pressure, Jigar was tempted to buy a larger home in Mumbai with an attractive view. Convinced he might "miss the opportunity," he withdrew his entire **₹1-crore** investment portfolio and stopped his SIPs to manage the new EMIs (Equated Monthly Instalments).

It was a classic case of emotion overpowering logic.

Their long-term financial freedom was disrupted—not by the market, but by a moment of panic masked as excitement.

"Discipline builds wealth; emotion destroys it."

Social and Cultural Influences:

Our money habits are not formed in isolation. They are shaped by family, peers, and society.

- **Cultural Norms:** In India, gold and property are often viewed as the safest investments because previous generations believed so.
- **Herd Mentality:** If everyone is investing in IPOs or a particular sector, we feel that we must follow.
- **Status-driven decisions:** Buying the latest LED television, iPhone, or SUV simply to signal success.

What worked for earlier generations does not necessarily work in today's financial landscape. Modern financial planning must consider new risks, opportunities, and lifestyle goals.

"It's not your salary that makes you rich, it's your money habits."

The Hidden Price Tag — No-Cost EMI & Cashback Deals

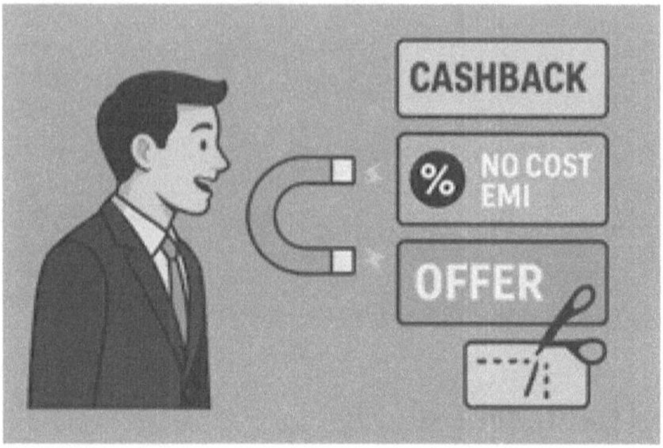

Marketing today is designed to make spending effortless. No-Cost EMIs and cashback schemes appear attractive, but they often contain hidden traps.

- **No-Cost EMI:** The interest is usually built into the product's final price. The customer pays more than they realise, and genuine discounts are typically withdrawn.
- **Cashbacks:** Often conditional
    1. Only valid on certain cards
    2. Credited after long delays
    3. Capped at small amounts
- **Up to 50% Off:** Retailers frequently inflate the original price to make the discount look larger.

- **Psychological Danger:** EMIs create the illusion of affordability. People buy things outside their budget simply because the monthly instalment 'looks manageable.'

"Buy what you truly need, buy within your budget, avoid falling for marketing illusions."

Client Story: The EMI Trap

Sandip, an IT professional in Pune earning ₹2 lakh per month, appeared financially secure from the outside.

But internally, he was overwhelmed.

His behaviours:

- Upgrading his iPhone every two years on EMI
- Purchasing a luxury car with a heavy loan despite his old one working well
- Dining out excessively
- Online shopping as a 'reward' for stress

Almost **60% of his salary** was going into EMIs and lifestyle expenses. Little remained for savings or investment.

With structured guidance, he:

- Built an emergency fund
- Stopped unnecessary EMIs

- Started goal-based SIPs
- Controlled lifestyle inflation

Eight years later, he invests more than **30%** of his income consistently and has built over **₹40 lakh** in financial assets.

Wealth isn't about what you earn, but how you behave with money.

Self-Check Quiz

Uncover your financial habits and hidden biases with this 2-minute quiz

Answer honestly. Pick the option that's closest to what you usually do.

1. **When the stock market falls by 15% in a few months, you…**

    a) Panic and sell to cut losses

    b) Hold on and wait it out

    c) See it as an opportunity to invest more.

2. **Your annual bonus arrives. What do you usually do?**

    a) Splurge it on gadgets, vacations, or shopping

    b) Keep some aside for savings, spend the rest

    c) Invest most of it towards future goals

3. **A new iPhone launches with "No-Cost EMI" of ₹4,000/month. You...**
   a) Grab it instantly — it's affordable in EMIs
   b) Think about it, maybe wait for discounts
   c) Skip it unless it fits into your budget/plan
4. **How often do you check your investment portfolio?**
   a) Daily—it stresses me if it's in red
   b) Monthly or quarterly for updates
   c) Only during periodic reviews or with an advisor
5. **Your neighbour just bought a luxury car. You feel...**
   a) Envious, tempted to upgrade too
   b) Curious, but not influenced
   c) Happy for them and focused on your own goals
6. **When you hear colleagues boasting of 30% returns in stocks...**
   a) You rush to invest in the same stocks
   b) You ask around but invest cautiously
   c) You stick to your plan and diversify
7. **What is your attitude towards credit cards?**
   a) Swipe freely; pay minimum dues later
   b) Use them but track bills
   c) Use carefully, clear dues in full every month

8. **If you suddenly got ₹10 lakhs, what would you do first?**

    a) Spend on lifestyle upgrades or luxury

    b) Split between spending and saving

    c) Allocate to investments and the emergency fund

9. **How do you decide on big-ticket purchases (car, house, vacation)?**

    a) Emotionally—because I deserve it!

    b) Compare deals and take an EMI/loan if affordable

    c) Align with financial plan and budget

10. **When it comes to retirement planning, you…**

    a) Haven't thought about it yet

    b) Save but without a clear plan

    c) Have a goal-based plan with SIPs/retirement corpus

Scoring:

- For each a) = 1 point
- For each b) = 2 points
- For each c) = 3 points

Results:

- **10–15 points → The Money Rookie**

Emotions and social pressure often guide your financial choices. You may fall into EMI and FOMO traps. But the good news: awareness is the first step to change.

- **16–24 points → The Smart Learner**

You balance logic with emotions. Sometimes you slip into biases, but you're improving. With discipline and guidance, you can achieve financial stability.

- **25–30 points → The Wealth Warrior**

You think long-term, avoid traps, and stay calm under pressure. You're on the right track—discipline, patience, and planning will help you achieve true freedom.

"There are no right or wrong answers. This quiz is to make you aware of your patterns. Awareness + action = transformation."

The 5 Behaviours That Build Wealth

1. **Live Below Your Means:** Spend less than you earn. Avoid lifestyle inflation even as your income grows.
2. **Pay Yourself First:** Treat saving and investing as a fixed monthly expense. Automate SIPs before spending.
3. **Practice Delay Gratification:** Ask yourself: Do I need this now, or can it wait? Pausing prevents impulsive decisions.
4. **Seek Expert Guidance:** Save time, avoid costly mistakes, and benefit from experience.
5. **Stay Consistent and Disciplined:** Wealth grows through patience, persistence, and steady action—not overnight.

"Money is 80% behaviour and 20% Skill." — ***Dave Ramsey.***

Key Learnings:

- **Know your biases:** Awareness allows control.
- **Separate emotion from decision:** Systems protect against impulsive mistakes.
- **Avoid lifestyle traps:** Peer pressure and instant gratification destroy wealth.
- **Beware of financial illusions:** No-Cost EMIs and cashback schemes are rarely as beneficial as they appear.
- **Stick to your goals:** Discipline and patience always outperform hype and trends.

"Wealth consists not in having great possessions, but in having few wants." – ***Epictetus.***

Chapter 5

The Spiritual Aspect of Money and Wealth

"It's not the man who has too little, but the man who craves more, that is poor."

— Seneca

The Deeper Connection

Money is often viewed as numbers, bank balances, and investments.

Yet, at a deeper level, money is energy — a medium that flows from one person to another, carrying intention, values, and impact. The way we earn, spend, save, and give reflects far more than financial choices; it reveals our beliefs, mindset, and inner world.

If health is wealth for the body, then the spiritual aspect of money is wealth for the soul. It reminds us that money is not the final destination, but a means to live a life of meaning, purpose, freedom, and contribution.

Wealth For a Balanced and Fulfilled Life

In ancient Indian philosophy, wealth was never confined to material prosperity; it was woven into a broader framework of **Dharma** (purpose), **Artha** (wealth), **Kama** (desire), and **Moksha** (liberation) — the four *purusharthas* that shape a meaningful life.

Artha was to be pursued in balance, guided by righteousness, clarity, and intention.

When money aligns with Dharma, everything shifts:

- Abundance flows naturally when our intentions are pure and generous.

- Fear and scarcity dissolve when we trust life's continuous flow.
- We use wealth consciously, creating joy for ourselves and others.

"Think of money as water: stagnant it stinks, hoarded it evaporates, but circulated it nurtures life."

When Artha Serves Dharma — The True Essence of Abundance

Not everyone is meant to be a yogi — someone who renounces the world to seek spiritual truth. But all of us can choose to be *Upyogi* — useful, purposeful, and conscious.

Being Upyogi means seeing money not merely as a means of consumption, but as a medium of contribution to family, community, and the world.

When wealth serves not just personal comfort but also a higher purpose, it becomes sacred.

धर्मेण अर्थः, अर्थेण आनन्दः

Dharmeṇa Arthaḥ, Artheṇa Ānandaḥ

"When Artha (wealth) aligns with Dharma (purpose), abundance transforms into Ananda (bliss)."

Reflection

Take a quiet moment to reflect:

- Is my wealth adding only comfort, or also meaning?
- How can my money serve a purpose beyond myself?

7 Energy Centres, 7 Levels of Freedom

At Adyanta Financials, we believe financial freedom unfolds in levels, much like life's energy centres.

Inspired by the concept of Financial Nirvana, our approach connects the **seven levels of financial freedom** with the **seven chakras** of the subtle energy body.

When aligned, money transforms from a source of stress into a source of strength, peace, and fulfilment.

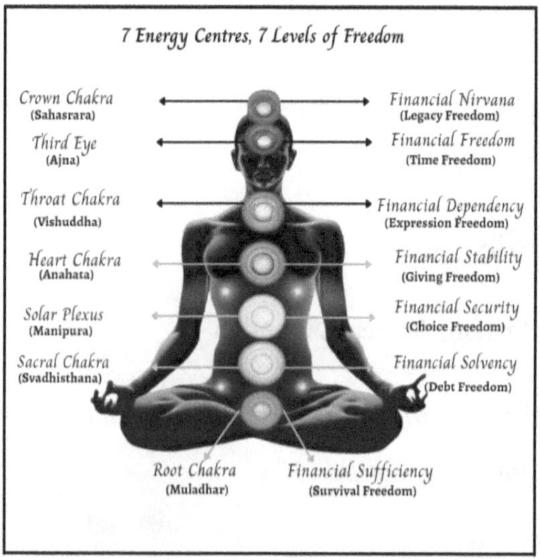

1. **Root Chakra (Muladhar) → Financial Sufficiency → Survival Freedom**

   Covering essential needs—food, shelter, health. No more pay cheque-to-pay cheque anxiety.

2. **Sacral Chakra (Svadhisthana) → Financial Solvency → Debt Freedom**

   Free from EMIs and credit traps. Money starts working for you.

3. **Solar Plexus (Manipura) → Financial Security → Choice Freedom**

   Confidence to say yes or no. Without fear. Spending, working, and investing with clarity.

4. **Heart Chakra (Anahata) → Financial Stability → Giving Freedom**

   The joy of abundance — sharing wealth, supporting family, contributing to causes.

5. **Throat Chakra (Vishuddha) → Financial Independence → Expression Freedom**

   Working authentically and pursuing one's passion without financial fear.

6. **Third Eye (Ajna) → Financial Freedom → Time Freedom**

   Assets buy back time. You live by purpose, not pay cheques.

7. **Crown Chakra (Sahasrara) → Financial Nirvana → Legacy Freedom**

   Your wealth outlives you. Values, contributions, and impact become your true currency.

Client Story: From Financial Solvency to Financial Independence

Aparna More, once an IT professional, felt drained by long hours and a repetitive routine. She was saving diligently but lacked direction in her investments and clarity about her future.

With guidance and a structured financial plan, Aparna not only gained financial security but also inner freedom. She discovered her true calling as a Yoga Therapist, dedicating her life to healing others.

Her story is a reminder that when managed wisely, money becomes more than security — it becomes a bridge to self-expression, purpose, and spiritual growth.

True wealth emerges when money aligns with one's purpose and meaning.

The Law of Giving

Many believe that giving reduces wealth. In truth, it expands it.

Giving — whether through donations, support, or even spending with gratitude — activates a powerful cycle of abundance. Money flows into someone else's growth. That person then contributes to another, and the cycle returns to you in unexpected ways: not always in currency, but in peace, goodwill, fulfilment, and opportunity.

At Adyanta, we encourage clients to ***give at least 5% of their income*** *— not after becoming wealthy, but while building wealth. Giving is not a reduction; it is an investment in humanity.*

Detachment and Discipline

Spirituality does not ask us to renounce money. It invites us to master our relationship with it.

- Do not become overly attached when markets rise.
- Do not lose yourself when they fall.
- Use discipline, gratitude, and balance as your anchors.

As the Bhagavad Gita teaches:

"You have the right to your actions, but not to the fruits thereof."

Applied to wealth, this means: focus on right effort, discipline, and intent — the results will follow naturally.

The Wealth of Purpose

Wealth is more than money. It is dignity, choices, freedom, and the ability to create impact. When wealth is tied merely to possessions, it feels shallow. When aligned with purpose — living fully, serving others, pursuing dreams — wealth becomes transformative.

Many of our clients began with financial goals but discovered genuine fulfilment only when their money started serving their life's purpose.

"Money fills your pockets. Purpose fills your Life."

Client Story: From Emptiness to Fullness

Ramesh, a senior corporate leader, once confided:

"Vipul, despite achieving more success and wealth than I ever imagined, I feel empty. My family is distant, my health is suffering, and I don't know why I'm working anymore."

Through coaching, he realised that his freedom did not lie in more wealth, but in aligned wealth. He began visiting NGOs, donating regularly, mentoring younger colleagues, and investing time in meaningful experiences with his family.

Within a year, his words changed from "I feel empty" to "I feel blessed and fulfilled."

"Wealth without purpose becomes a burden; with purpose it becomes freedom."

Practical Ways to Bring Spirituality into Wealth

1. **Practice Gratitude** — Pause before spending and appreciate what you have.
2. **Give consistently** — Support causes that resonate with your heart.
3. **Align with Purpose** — Choose what brings lasting value, not momentary pleasure.
4. **Detach from Outcomes** — Focus on the right process, not just returns.
5. **Live More, Give More** — Make generosity part of your financial plan.

Key Learnings:

1. **Money is energy** — its flow is more important than its accumulation.
2. **Giving doesn't reduce wealth;** it expands it.
3. **True financial freedom** is not about having more, but **being more.**
4. **Discipline and detachment** form the foundation of emotional and financial stability.
5. **When aligned with spirituality, it becomes a tool for purpose, peace, prosperity,** and legacy.

"Wealth is not what you keep, but what you give, create, and leave behind."

PILLAR 2

PROTECT & PREPARE

Secure your foundation with budgeting, insurance, family conversations, women's wealth, and tax planning.

Chapter 6

Budgeting— The First Step to Wealth and Freedom

"Do not save what is left after spending; instead spend what is left after saving."

— Warren Buffett

"Most people don't lose money because they don't earn enough — they lose it because they don't manage it well."

Sounds familiar?

If you've ever thought, "Where did my money go?" — this chapter is for you.

Why Budgeting Matters — Even for High Earners

Even those earning ₹5 lakhs a month often end up paycheck-to-paycheck—spending to impress or embracing the 'Zindagi Na Milegi Dobara' mantra of living only for today. Wealth grows from managing income well, not just earning more.

"Income isn't the problem — unplanned spending is."

Client Story: From Empty Pockets to Purposeful Investing

A tech couple in Bengaluru earning ₹3 lakhs per month approached Adyanta, feeling overwhelmed by rising credit-card debt and scattered expenses.

We introduced them to two simple actions:

1. **Follow the 40:30:30 Rule**
    - 40% → Needs and lifestyle

- 30% → Investments (via SIPs)
- 30% → EMIs

2. **Automate their monthly SIPs (Systematic Investment Plans) to ensure savings happen before spending.**

In six months, they built a ₹6-lakh emergency fund by consistently saving ₹1 lakh per month. Today, they are investing purposefully towards their top three financial goals.

Budgeting gave them clarity, control, and confidence.

Adyanta's Smart Budgeting Rules

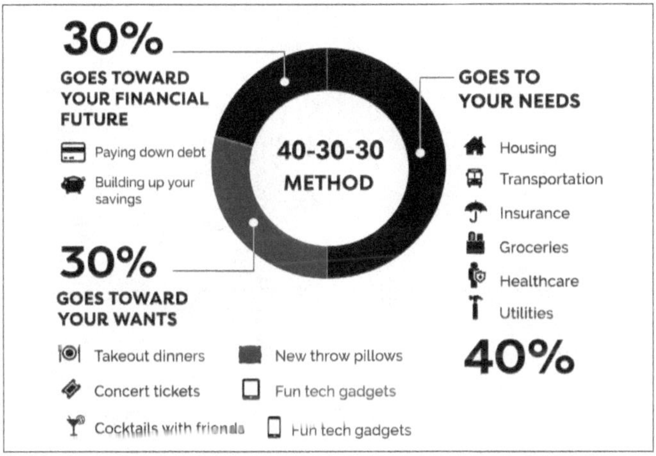

- **40:30:30 Rule** — 40% for needs & lifestyle, 30% for goals (SIPs), 30% for EMIs
- **50:30:20 (If No EMIs)** — 50% needs, 30% goals, 20% dreams (such as a bigger house or early retirement)

- **Automate your SIPs** — save first, spend what's left

"A budget doesn't limit your freedom; it gives you freedom." — Rachel Cruze.

Client Story: From Chaos to Control

Akash and Pranita, a young couple from Nashik earning ₹2 lakhs per month, wanted financial discipline and clarity. Their goals included an annual holiday, a car for weekend getaways, and purchasing a home.

After a clarity call and a discovery session, we refined their priorities:

1. **Buy a home within five years**
2. **Take one planned annual holiday**

Our recommendations:

- Allocate no more than 10% of monthly income (₹20,000) for travel
- Delay the car purchase for five years — use app-based rentals instead
- Start a ₹25,000 monthly SIP towards the home down-payment

The outcome:

After four years, they had:

- **₹14 lakhs** for a home down-payment
- **₹2 lakhs** in an emergency fund
- **Zero debt**

They gained clarity, direction, and discipline — the core of financial freedom.

"Budgeting is the first step in achieving financial stability."

Creating a Simple Household Budget

1. Write down your monthly inflow and outflow — no app, just paper
2. Categorise expenses into: Needs, Goals, EMIs, Lifestyle.
3. Automate Goal-based SIPs of at least 20–30% of your income.
4. Set a 3-month goal: Reduce wasteful spending by a minimum of ₹5,000.
5. Create an emergency fund equal to 3 to 6 months' expenses.

"The best time to budget was when you got your first salary. The second-best time is now."

Budgeting Mistakes to Avoid

1. Budgeting once a year and then forgetting about it
2. Treating bonuses as 'free money.'
3. Ignoring the emergency fund
4. Lifestyle upgrades after appraisals

"Budgeting isn't about saying no — it's about saying yes to what truly matters."

Client Story: From Income to Impact

The Sharma family earned well but struggled to save. EMIs, weekend outings, credit-card spending, and their son's hobby classes took up nearly **70% of their income.**

With a structured budgeting framework, they redirected **30% of their income** to investments. Suddenly, their dreams — their son's education, a better home, and a secure retirement — no longer felt distant.

Their lifestyle improved, not because they earned more, but because they **became conscious of how they allocated their income.**

"It's not what you earn, but what you allocate, that shapes your financial future."

Key Learnings:

1. High income without a plan leads to financial leaks.
2. Budgeting is a mindset tool, not just a spreadsheet.
3. Use simple rules like 40:30:30 or 50:30:20.
4. Big expenses — holidays, cars, homes — must be planned, not impulsive.
5. Automation is the easiest way to build long-term consistency.

Chapter 7

First Shield, Then Sword — Insurance & Protection

"Preparation is the key to success."

— Alexander Graham Bell

"You don't buy insurance because you're going to die. You buy it because your loved ones will live."

Before you invest, before you chase returns, you must secure your foundation. A strong financial plan always begins with protection.

Why People Delay Insurance — And the Cost of Delay

Many individuals postpone buying insurance because of psychological biases, financial misconceptions, or simply a lack of awareness.

The truth? Delaying by even five years can significantly increase your premiums — or worse, make you uninsurable.

Buying insurance while you are young and healthy maximises your chances of approval and ensures the lowest possible cost with the best terms.

Client Story: Delay Doesn't Just Cost, It Multiplies

Samir began his SIPs (Systematic Investment Plans) of ₹50,000 for his major life goals at age 37, but he kept postponing the ₹1 Crore Term Plan we recommended.

By the time he finally acted at 44 — after being diagnosed with Type 1 diabetes — his premium had jumped from ₹12,000 to ₹38,000 due to age and health loading.

"The best time to buy insurance was yesterday. The next best is now."

Non-Negotiable Covers

- **Term Insurance:** Minimum cover of 10 times your annual income.

- **Health Insurance:** A ₹10 Lakh family floater policy.
- **Personal Accident:** Especially crucial for young earners.
- **Critical Illness:** Recommended if there is a family history of severe illnesses.
- **Home Insurance:** Covers fire, theft, earthquakes, and other natural calamities.

Client Story: Protection in a Crisis

Amar Patil, a 49-year-old executive from Thane, passed away unexpectedly in 2019 due to cardiac arrest. He had a ₹1 Crore Term Plan along with a ₹50 Lakh Group Term Life cover from his employer. His wife, Asmita — a homemaker at the time — did not have to compromise her lifestyle or worry about their daughter's future education.

Today, Asmita is a professional artist exhibiting in renowned galleries across the world. Her financial goals remain on track, exactly as planned.

ULIP vs Term + MF – What's Better?

A pure Term Insurance plan provides high coverage at a low cost. For instance, the premium for a ₹1 Crore term policy for a 30-year-old, non-smoking, healthy male in India is approximately ₹10,000–12,000 per year.

ULIPs (Unit Linked Insurance Plans), on the other hand, combine investment and insurance, which often results in lower coverage.

However, certain low-cost ULIPs such as *ICICI Pru Protect N Gain,* which offer life cover up to 125 times the annual premium, may be considered — but only for younger individuals aged 25 to 35.

A combination of Term Insurance and a low-cost ULIP may work for young adults needing high coverage with flexibility. Beyond age 40, however, Term Insurance remains the best shield against untimely death.

"Protection is not optional. It's the foundation."

Would you wear a shirt smaller than your size?

Of course not. It would feel tight, uncomfortable, and ill-fitted.

Yet many people make this exact mistake with insurance — they buy a policy that is too "small" for their family's needs.

The right fit matters.

Think of Term Insurance as that shirt: if it does not suit your life stage, income, and responsibilities, it cannot protect your family properly.

Many proudly say, "I already have term insurance."

But once we analyse the numbers, their coverage is often nowhere near sufficient.

"Being underinsured is like wearing a shirt two sizes smaller — it looks like you've covered yourself, but the discomfort shows up when life tests you."

What is Human Life Value (HLV) and why is it Important?

HLV represents your exact financial worth to your family.

It answers one important question:

"If I am not here, how much money will my family need to maintain their lifestyle and meet future goals?"

HLV is used by financial planners to determine the right amount of life cover required to:

maintain the family's standard of living,

meet short-term and long-term goals, and

repay outstanding loans.

The 2 common approaches to calculating the Human Life Value are:

- **Income Replacement:** Consider your total future earnings until retirement.
- **Need-Based:** Considers goals, liabilities, daily expenses, and lifestyle needs.

*At **Adyanta,** we use the **Need-Based method,** as it is personalised, comprehensive, and precise in covering recommendations.*

Client Story: A Wake-Up Call

Sandeep Mestry, a young industrialist from Mumbai, never took insurance seriously — until he lost a close friend to a sudden heart attack. Watching the family struggle financially was a turning point.

Sandeep immediately purchased term insurance for himself and his wife, Supriya, based on their Human Life Value.

For him, it was no longer about buying a policy; it was about securing peace of mind.

"Don't wait for a wake-up call. Protect your family today."

Insurance Done Right: Common Mistakes to Avoid

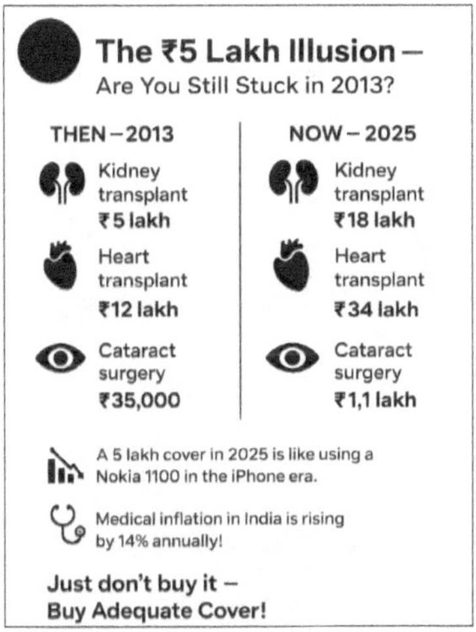

Insurance is not merely a product; it is a responsibility. Yet many people make mistakes that reduce protection or increase costs:

- Relying solely on a company's Group Term cover or holding multiple traditional policies with inadequate coverage.
- Buying insurance from friends or relatives without proper research.
- Skipping annual policy reviews or delaying renewals.
- Choosing ULIPs or "Return of Premium" plans purely for protection.
- Buying health insurance online or frequently porting policies only to save costs.

Client Story: When Health Struck, Insurance Saved

Siddhesh Keluskar, a young professional from Mumbai, resigned from his company after securing a better opportunity. Before he could join the new firm, he suffered a heart attack.

In those stressful days, one thing he did not have to worry about was money — his personal health insurance covered all hospital expenses.

Had he relied only on his company's group cover, he would have been left uninsured between jobs, forced to dip into his savings, and compromise his future goals.

"Your job can change, but your protection shouldn't. Own your health cover — it's your safety net beyond employment."

Selecting the Right Health and Life Protection Plan

Once you know the amount of life cover and health cover required for your family, assess the following:

1. **Claim settlement ratio** – 98%+ for life insurance and 85% + for health insurance.
2. **Optional Riders** – For example, an Accidental Death Rider for life insurance.
3. **Cashless hospital network**, pre- and post-hospitalisation coverage, and no-claim bonus in case of health insurance.

4. **Features such as no capping,** Maternity benefit (whether needed or not), etc. – in case of health insurance, and **Increasing Life Coverage**, Limited payment options, etc – in case of life insurance.
5. Brand and Size of company, **Quality and Speed of Service,** and finally the costs.

Your 5-Step Protection Checklist

1. **Know your Human Life Value (HLV)** before deciding on term cover.
2. **Base health insurance** on your income, lifestyle, and medical needs.
3. **Add essential riders** like accidental, critical illness, and waiver of premium.
4. **Keep nominees and contact details updated** to avoid future disputes.

5. **Disclose medical history honestly** and review policies annually.

"The cost of not having insurance is always greater than the premium you pay."

Key Learnings:

1. **Protection is your first step** — not investments.
2. **Seek help from a Trusted Professional** to choose the right coverage and product.
3. **Buy when you are healthy. Don't delay** — health issues can make you uninsurable.
4. **Employer insurance is not enough** — buy your own.
5. **Insurance gives your family** time to recover, not just money.

Chapter 8

Money is a Family Affair — Build Together, Live Together

"The strength of a nation derives from the integrity of the family."

— Confucius

"If money affects the whole family, why is only one person making all the decisions?"

Money conversations are often skipped at home — yet they affect every member of the family.

In this chapter, we explore why involving your family in financial decisions builds clarity, confidence, and deeper trust.

Why Talk Money as a Family?

Money touches everyone — spouse, kids, even ageing parents. Yet many households avoid discussing it due to discomfort, fear of judgment, or long-standing habits.

When you involve your family, you get alignment, support, and most importantly — trust.

"Money is emotional. Talk about it before it becomes a source of stress."

Client Story: From Chaos to Clarity

When Rutaa Kothare lost her husband, her world collapsed overnight.

He had always managed the finances, rarely involving the family. Rutaa, although working, remained distant from the financial aspects. He left behind investments, but without a roadmap.

Grief was overwhelming, and the confusion added to her loneliness. Together, we structured her finances — building a plan that provided steady income, clarity, and the confidence to stand tall again.

Today, Rutaa ensures her daughter, Arpita, is involved in every financial decision, determined to raise her with both **security and independence.**

Joint vs Separate — What's Ideal?

- Joint accounts for shared goals: home, education, retirement.
- Separate accounts for autonomy and individual choices.
- 70:30 rule — 70% joint, 30% personal works well for most couples.

"Joint decisions lead to stronger outcomes."

Teaching Kids Money Skills Early

Financial education must start before algebra. Children learn far more from exposure and habits than from lectures. Start with allowances and teach saving-spending-giving.

- Provide allowances and teach the **save–spend–give** method.
- Open a **junior bank account** with you as the guardian.
- Introduce simple concepts such as the **Time Value of Money, inflation, and compounding** (how money grows when returns earn further returns).
- Share family goals in simple terms—make them feel included.
- Lead by example — children mirror financial habits more than words.

"Transparency in finance builds trust in relationships."

5 Red Flags — Joint or Blended Family

1. **Lack of Transparency** — Hidden incomes, debts, or expenses create mistrust and financial stress.
2. **Unequal Contribution** — When money responsibilities aren't fairly shared, resentment builds up.
3. **Overdependence** — Relying too much on one earning member makes the family financially fragile.

4. **Conflicting Priorities** — Differing goals (home, education, lifestyle) can derail overall planning.
5. **Avoiding Money Talks** — Silence around finances leads to misunderstandings and poor decisions.

Client Story: From Debt to Direction

A doctor couple from Pune had mortgaged their bungalow and taken loans to build their hospital. The husband, solely managing finances, felt excluded, leading to stress and conflict.

Through a joint family session, we created a shared financial folder, updated nominees, and built a roadmap. This restored trust, gave clarity, and set them on track to expand their hospital, reduce debt, and invest confidently for the future. A doctor couple from Pune had mortgaged their bungalow and taken loans to build their hospital.

With the husband managing finances alone, the wife felt excluded, leading to stress and conflict.

During a joint family session, we created:

- A shared financial folder,
- Updated nominees,
- A structured roadmap for debt reduction and growth.

This restored trust, brought clarity, and set them on the path to expand their hospital, reduce debt, and invest confidently.

During a recent review, the wife shared, *"Now I don't just feel financially safe — I feel included."*

Your 5-Step Family Finance Action Plan

1. **Create a Family Finance Folder** — include investments, loans, insurance, and passwords.
2. **Conduct a quarterly 'Money Talk'** with your spouse/ family.
3. **Add or update nominees** in all financial instruments as and when necessary.
4. **Empower women** in the family to manage the household budget; they are extremely good at it.
5. **Build a Money Team at Home** — Do not manage money in isolation; share responsibility.

Key Learnings:

1. Money silence in families leads to future confusion.
2. Joint + separate finances give balance and clarity.
3. Kids need money for education, not just academic pressure.
4. Nomination and documentation are as important as investing.
5. Inclusion creates emotional and financial safety.

Chapter 9

Women & Wealth – The Untold Story

"Lasting net worth comes only when you have a healthy and strong sense of self-worth"

— Suze Orman

"Financial independence is not a luxury. It's a life skill every woman must have."

This chapter is a call to action for every woman — and for every family that truly values long-term security and dignity.

Why It's Non-Negotiable

Even today, millions of educated and capable women remain financially dependent on their spouses or parents. Many working women still rely on someone else to make their financial decisions.

Life events such as career breaks, divorce, illness, or caregiving responsibilities can leave women financially vulnerable.

Freedom isn't just about rights — **it's about access to resources, control, and informed decision-making.**

"Financial independence is the foundation of personal freedom."

How Homemakers Can Build Wealth

Homemakers devote themselves to building stable families — they deserve equal dignity, confidence, and financial independence.

- Manage the household budget efficiently— to create regular savings
- Invest the household savings, side income, or gift money

- Empower with financial knowledge, engage in family goals
- Start small — even ₹1,000/month SIP to build wealth over time
- Use Bank FDs or short-term debt funds for emergency or short-term needs

"Money in your name is power in your hands."

Client Story: From Uncertainty to Empowerment

Smita Patil, a homemaker from Powai, had devoted herself to her family, placing complete trust in her husband to manage their finances.

A decade ago, life took an unexpected turn. As a single mother of two young sons, she was left with a house and ₹1 crore from an out-of-court settlement — but little clarity about how to secure her family's future.

Together, we crafted a financial roadmap that preserved her independence, safeguarded her children's education, and helped her rebuild with confidence.

Today, Smita stands tall — her elder son is an engineer at a leading MNC, and her younger one is preparing for IIT. Her journey reflects not loss, but the quiet power of resilience, awareness, and informed choices.

"Empowered women build empowered futures."

Why Working Women Must Aim for Financial Independence

For many working women, the pursuit of higher income is seen as the ultimate financial goal. While earning more certainly enhances lifestyle and security, true empowerment lies not just in the size of one's paycheck but in achieving **financial independence.**

Financial independence means having the knowledge, confidence, and control to make informed money decisions without depending on a spouse, family member, or employer. It's about building assets, protecting risks, and ensuring that your future choices remain yours alone.

Why this shift matters:

- **Income ≠ Independence:** A high salary without savings, investments, or protection still leads to dependence.
- **Life is unpredictable:** Marriage, career breaks, or health challenges can disrupt income streams. Independence cushions the impact.
- **Freedom of choice:** Financially independent women can pursue passions, change careers, or take sabbaticals without fear.
- **Generational impact:** Women who manage money confidently inspire the next generation to do the same.

"Earning more adds comfort, but financial independence ensures dignity, security, and freedom."

Client Story: From Financial Security to Purposeful Freedom

After a successful and fulfilling corporate career, Vinu Pillai, an HR professional from Thane, had achieved most of her planned milestones. Yet, an inner voice urged her toward something more — a desire to create impact and build something that truly reflected her values and vision.

That's when financial clarity and disciplined planning with Adyanta Financials became the turning point. With a well-structured roadmap and renewed confidence, Vinu took the bold leap into entrepreneurship, launching Vinicio Advisory, her global consulting venture.

Her journey is a testament to how financial independence can empower women to design their own path — with courage, purpose, and freedom.

"Financial independence isn't just about numbers; it's about the freedom to choose your next chapter with confidence."

5-Step Starter Kit for Working Women

1. **Start goal-based SIPs** — in your name.

2. **Buy your own term cover** — and a health cover in the absence of a family floater
3. **Create a personal emergency fund** of 3 to 6 months' outflows.

4. **Track and review** your investments periodically— at least once a year.
5. **Discuss and document your financial rights** in family assets.
6. **Invest in Knowledge** — Learn and stay updated to make smarter money decisions.
7. **Plan your Retirement early** — The earlier you save and invest, the freer you retire.

"Every working woman deserves to have a Plan B — and a Plan Wealth."

Key Learnings:

1. Financial Empowerment for women is essential, not optional.
2. Homemakers can invest too — every small step counts.
3. Working women must secure their wealth and protection.
4. Mental barriers are real — but can be broken with clarity.
5. Empowered women lead empowered families.

Chapter 10

Protect What You Earn— Tax Planning That Works

"In this world nothing can be said to be certain, except death and taxes."

— Benjamin Franklin

"It's not how much you make; it's how much you keep that counts."
— Robert Kiyosaki.

The new tax regime is now the default income tax option in India, offering lower tax rates in exchange for forgoing most deductions and exemptions.

For the 2025–2026 financial year, the basic exemption limit has been increased to ₹4 lakh, and the tax rebate has been enhanced to make income up to ₹12 lakh tax-free.

Old Regime vs New Regime — What Should You Choose?

The New Regime (as per Union Budget 2025-26) offers:

- Lower tax rates across slabs
- Simplicity: No complex proofs or deductions
- ₹75,000 Standard deduction for Salaried Employees and Zero Tax on Annual Income up to ₹ 12.75 Lakhs

- 30% Standard deduction on the Net Annual Value (NAV) of a rented property in India
- Full interest deduction (No upper limit) on home loan for let-out property
- Employer contributions up to 14% of your basic salary in EPF/NPS (up to ₹ 7.5 Lakhs per year) u/s 80 CCD (2)

However, if you're someone who is earning over Rs. 12.75 Lakhs from Salary:

And your Total deductions — including Housing Rent Allowance (HRA), u/s 80C, u/s 80D, LTA, home loan interest payments, and NPS — exceed ₹4.25 Lakhs, then the old tax regime can be more beneficial.

Otherwise, the New Regime could give you more flexibility and less paperwork.

"The choice between the new and old regimes depends on your income and eligible deductions."

Long Term Capital Gains on Property (LTCG)

The LTCG tax is levied on profits from the sale of property in India if the property is held for more than 24 months. If the holding period is less than 24 months, the gains are added to the total income for the year and taxed according to the individual income tax slab rate.

- For properties acquired on or before July 22, 2024, there are 2 options to calculate the LTCG Tax:

    1. **12.5% without indexation** — with this option, you cannot adjust the inflation price.
    2. **20% with indexation** — with this option, you can adjust the price for inflation using the Cost-Of-Living Index (CII)

- For Properties acquired on or after July 23, 2024, the tax rate for LTCG is flat 12.5%.

Section 54 EC — Deduction on LTCG through Capital Gain Bonds

The LTCG tax can be avoided by re-investing the LTCG into:

- Another property (one year before or 2 years after the date of transfer of the old house)
- Construction of a house within a period of 3 years from the date of transfer
- NHAI or REC Bonds under Section 54 EC (Up to ₹50 lakhs with 5 years locking, annualised 5.25% interest) within 6 months from the date of transfer of property

Should You Use Section 54 EC? Let's learn through the client story below.

Client Story: Pay Tax or Use 54EC

Mridula sold a property with ₹40 Lakhs LTCG. Under the new regime, her tax was ₹6.25 Lakhs. She had two choices—invest ₹50 Lakhs in REC Bonds at 5.25% for 5 years, or pay tax and reinvest ₹43.75 Lakhs at ~10% CAGR.

We guided her to choose the latter, which proved ₹5+ Lakhs better.

If you're risk-averse, 54EC works, but if you can earn >10% post-tax returns, paying LTCG tax and reinvesting delivers superior long-term returns.

Section 54F: Turning Capital Gains into a Home

When you sell a long-term capital asset—like gold, shares, or land (other than a house)—the profit, i.e., **LTCG, is taxable.** Section 54F offers a way to save this tax by reinvesting the **net sale proceeds** in a **residential house** in India.

Key Rules:

- Timeline: Buy within 1 year before or 2 years after, or construct within 3 years.
- Ownership: You must not own more than one house (excluding the new one).
- Full/Partial Investment: Exemption is full if you reinvest all proceeds; partial if only part is invested.

- Lock-in: Don't sell the new house within 3 years.

Smart Usage:

- Deposit proceeds in a Capital Gains Account Scheme (CGAS) if not reinvesting immediately.
- Pick a property that suits your long-term plans, since you must hold it for at least 3 years.

"Section 54F helps you legally cut taxes while converting gains into a lasting asset—a home."

Tax Harvesting: Turning Losses into Tax Savings

When it comes to investing, taxes can quietly eat into your returns. One smart way to minimise this impact is through **tax harvesting**—also called **tax-loss harvesting.** At its core, it's a strategy where you sell investments that are currently at a loss to offset the gains from other investments. By doing so, you reduce your taxable income and ultimately lower the tax you pay.

How Does It Work?

For mutual fund investors, tax harvesting is straightforward:

1. **Spot the Losses** – Identify mutual fund units that are currently valued lower than your purchase price.
2. **Sell the Units** – Book those losses by selling the identified units.

3. **Offset the Gains** - Use these booked losses to reduce taxable gains from other mutual fund redemptions.
4. **Reinvest** - Redirect the proceeds into another suitable mutual fund in the same financial year to keep your portfolio aligned with your goals.

For equity investors, tax harvesting is the practice of selling loss-making shares to reduce the tax on their profits, and then reinvesting to keep their portfolio on track in the same financial year.

Why Should You Consider It?

- **Tax Savings** - Reduces taxable income, leaving more money in your hands.
- **Better Net Returns** - Lower taxes mean higher effective returns over time.
- **Long-Term Advantage** - Consistent application can create meaningful savings that compound over the years.

Client Story: Turning Tax Savings into Joy

The Gupta family used to save ₹20,000 a month in a Bank RD for their annual vacation. When we analysed their cash flows, taxes, and investments, we realised that they were not planning their taxes or optimising their taxes.

We suggested — tax-harvesting ₹1.25 Lakhs every year from their mutual fund portfolio, saving ₹31,250 in LTCG tax.

Now, their vacations continue as before, while the tax savings fund their shopping.

Don't let compounding be eaten by tax you could've avoided.

Presumptive Taxation Made Simple – Section 44AD

For small businesses, maintaining books and facing tax audits can be cumbersome. Section 44AD offers a simplified route by allowing taxpayers to declare income at a fixed percentage of turnover instead of actual profits.

Who Can Opt In?

Resident individuals, HUFs, and partnership firms (not LLPs).

Turnover Limits:

- Up to ₹2 crore if cash receipts exceed 5% of turnover.
- Up to ₹3 crore if 95%+ receipts are digital.

How It Works:

- 8% of turnover (cash receipts).
- 6% of turnover (digital receipts).
- No separate deductions or depreciation claims.

Not Eligible:

- **Professionals (44ADA):** Doctors, lawyers, consultants, etc., can declare 50% of gross receipts as taxable income (subject to limits and conditions).
- **Commission Agents & Transporters (44AE):** Eligible to declare fixed income (per vehicle, per month) or as per prescribed norms instead of maintaining full books.

Key Rules:

- File using ITR-4.
- Pay advance tax by 15th March.
- **Must continue for 5 years once opted;** early exit bars re-entry for the next 5 years (unless turnover crosses ₹3 crore).

"Section 44AD is a convenient, stress-free, and time-saving option for small businesses, but with conditions—choose wisely."

Inheritance and Taxes: What You Really Need to Know

Inheritance may come with emotions, but it also raises tax questions. The truth is simple: **receiving an inheritance is tax-free in India,** but what you do with it later is what gets taxed.

No Tax on Inheritance

India does not levy an inheritance tax. Assets passed on through a will or inheritance are fully exempt under the Income Tax Act, 1961.

Tax on Income from Inherited Assets

The assets may be tax-free, but income from them isn't.

- **Rental Income:** Taxed under "Income from House Property".
- **Interest Income:** Taxed as "Income from Other Sources".
- **Dividends:** Taxable, as per applicable income tax slab rates.

"Inheritance itself is tax-free, but earnings and capital gains from it are taxable."

Capital Gains on Sale

Selling inherited assets attracts capital gains tax:

- The original purchase price (by the person you inherit from) is taken as your cost.
- Their holding period counts toward short- or long-term classification. (<24 or >24 months)
- Gains are taxed as per asset-specific rules.

Example: *If your father bought property in 1990 and you sell it in 2025, the indexed cost since 1990 applies, and gains are taxed as long-term capital gains.*

Smart Tax Hacks for the New Tax Regime

1. **Tax-free perks for Salaried People** — Use employer-provided benefits (LTA, food coupons, mobile reimbursement, as per the eligibility limits).
2. **Choose Corporate NPS** — If offered by your Company for tax deduction u/s 80 CCD (2) *
3. **For Professionals and Transport Agents** — shift to presumptive taxation if eligible
4. **Use tax harvesting across asset classes** — equity, gold, real estate, or debt (short term against short term and long term against long term)
5. **Carry forward unadjusted losses** to a future year to offset the taxable gains in the future. **

** Max limit = ₹ 7.50 Lakhs on employer contribution.*

*** The specific rules, eligibility, and time limits depend on the type of loss and tax.*

Key Learnings:

1. **Evaluate yearly** — regime choice, capital gains, and tax-saving opportunities
2. **Capital Gains taxes can be minimised**— with proper knowledge and timely execution

3. **Tax harvesting is not about avoiding taxes,** but about being tax-smart.
4. **Tax Strategies** such as loss harvesting or 54EC **should be applied thoughtfully** in alignment with your broader financial goals.
5. **Always consult a qualified financial advisor** before implementing a tax strategy, to ensure the strategy suits your personal situation and complies with the latest tax regulations.

"Paying tax is patriotic. Overpaying it isn't."

PILLAR 3

GROW & ALLOCATE

With protection in place, it's time to grow. Smart allocation, goal-based investing, and disciplined reviews help you create wealth with confidence.

Chapter 11

Understanding Your Risk Profile — And Why Time Horizon Matters

"Risk comes from not knowing what you're doing."

— Warren Buffett.

Every financial decision you make—whether investing in equities, buying property, or even choosing insurance—comes with a degree of risk. But the way you perceive and handle that risk is unique.

Some people panic at the slightest market dip, while others stay calm even in a crash. That difference lies in your **risk profile**—a blend of your financial situation, goals, and psychology.

Understanding it is crucial because it ensures you invest in a way that feels comfortable, sustainable, and aligned with your long-term objectives.

When your investments match your risk appetite, you're less likely to make emotional mistakes and more likely to stay the course on your wealth journey.

Your investment risk profile

It is a blend of:

- Your emotional tolerance for market swings
- Your financial capacity to absorb losses
- And most importantly, your investment time horizon

Why Time Horizon Trumps Risk Appetite

Most people say they are "conservative" or "aggressive." But your time horizon should dictate your risk—not your mood.

- **Short-term goal** (0–3 years)? Capital protection matters. Debt or liquid funds make sense.
- **Medium-term** (3–7 years)? Balanced allocation with some equity exposure.
- **Long-term** (>7 years)? Equity is your best friend.

Client Story: Time Turns Volatility into Wealth

Sanjay, 30, wanted to start saving for retirement 25 years away. We advised him to allocate 100% towards equity toward this goal, with an SIP of ₹ 20,000/- pm. In an equity mutual fund.

Today, after 10 years, his Retirement Corpus has grown to over ₹ 53 Lakhs at a CAGR of 14.5%, much higher than his expectation.

By leveraging time, his portfolio has grown far more than a conservative mix would have delivered.

What are Risk-Adjusted Returns?

Investment return alone means nothing without risk. Two funds with the same returns may carry vastly different volatility.

Risk-Adjusted Return = How much return you get per unit of risk taken.

The common risk-adjusted return metrics used to compare mutual funds:

- **Standard Deviation** → Measures how much the fund's returns fluctuate (volatility).
- **Sharpe Ratio** → Shows how much extra return the fund generates for every unit of risk taken.
- **Sortino Ratio** → Similar to Sharpe but only considers downside risk (bad volatility).
- **Beta** → Indicates how sensitive the fund is to market movements (1 = moves with the market).
- **Alpha** → Extra return the fund manager generates compared to the market benchmark after adjusting for risk.
- **R-Squared (R^2)** → Tells how closely the fund's performance is linked to its benchmark (higher = more aligned).
- **Treynor Ratio** → Shows return generated per unit of market risk (systematic risk via Beta).

Types of Investment Risks

Not all risks are about market crashes. The key types of risk include:

- **Inflation Risk:** The danger that rising prices will erode your money's purchasing power.
- **Volatility Risk:** The risk of sharp ups and downs in investment value due to market swings.
- **Concentration Risk:** The risk of losses from investing too heavily in one asset, sector, or theme.

- **Liquidity Risk:** The difficulty of converting investments into cash quickly without a loss.
- **Interest Rate Risk:** The chance of bond or debt investment values falling when interest rates rise.
- **Reinvestment Risk:** The risk of future returns being lower when reinvested at prevailing rates.
- **Diversification Risk** (Over-diversification): The risk of diluting returns by spreading investments too thin.

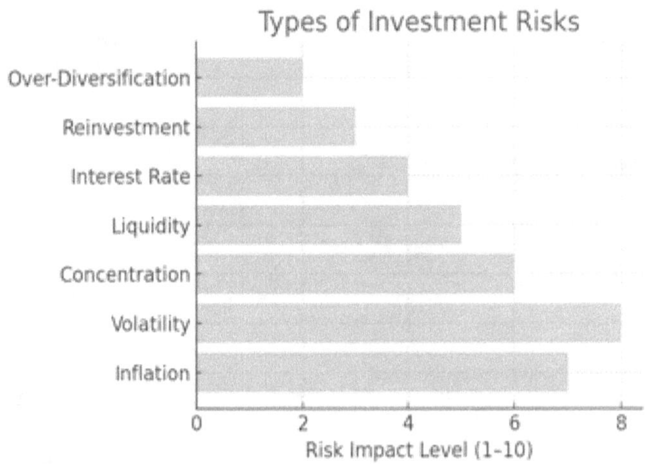

Client Story: Balancing Risk and Return

Rohit, a 42-year-old IT professional, was proud of his aggressive investment portfolio—mostly mid- and small-cap stocks. The returns looked spectacular in good years, but whenever the market dipped, his portfolio crashed, leaving him anxious and sleepless.

When he engaged us, we introduced him to the concept of risk-adjusted returns. Instead of chasing the highest returns, we rebalanced his portfolio to include a mix of equity, debt, and gold. While his overall returns appeared slightly lower on paper compared to his earlier "all-in" approach, the ride became far smoother.

Rohit realised that true wealth isn't about the **highest return**, but the **best possible return for the level of risk you can comfortably handle.**

"It's not about chasing the highest return—it's about earning the right risk-adjusted return."

Visualising Risk vs Return

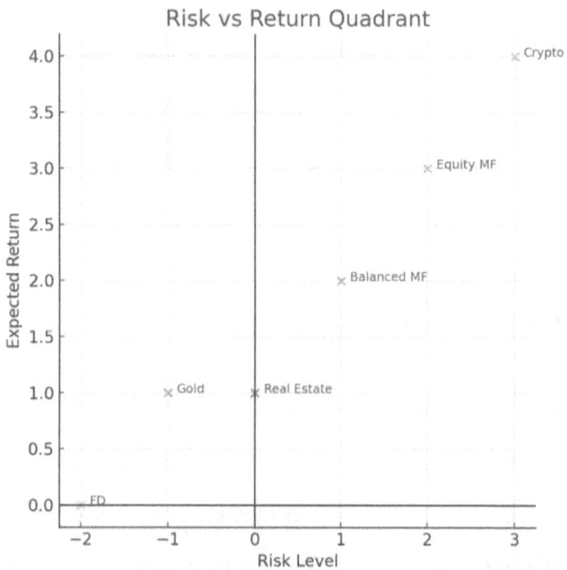

Risk Appetite vs. Risk Tolerance

Risk Appetite is the willingness to take risks. It's how much volatility or uncertainty an investor is comfortable with while pursuing returns. (E.g., "I'm okay with market ups and downs if it means higher long-term growth.")

Risk Tolerance is the ability to take risks. It depends on financial capacity, goals, income stability, age, and commitments. (E.g., "Even if I want to take risks, my financial situation may or may not allow it.")

"Appetite is what your mind wants, tolerance is what your pocket allows."

Client Story: Rohit's Investment Journey

Rohit, 32, a young IT professional, always said, *"I love high-risk investments. I want to double my money fast."* His risk appetite was very high.

But when we reviewed his finances, we found he had home loan EMIs, young children, and no emergency fund. His risk tolerance was actually low — his financial base wasn't strong enough to handle big losses.

With coaching, he first built a safety net, created a disciplined SIP plan, and allocated only a small portion to aggressive investments.

Over time, his portfolio became both growth-oriented and stable.

"True wealth is created when your risk appetite aligns with your risk tolerance."

Self-Check Quiz: Understanding Your Risk Profile

Answer the following honestly. Circle the option that resonates most with you.

1. **If your investment of ₹5 lakhs drops to ₹4.25 lakhs in 6 months, you would...**

   a) Withdraw immediately to avoid further loss

   b) Wait for a year to see if it recovers

   c) Stay invested and even add more if possible

2. **When investing, what matters most to you?**

   a) Safety of capital

   b) Balance of growth and safety

   c) Maximum possible growth over time

3. **Which statement feels closest to your approach?**

   a) "I hate losing money—even small amounts."

   b) "I can take some risks if it helps me grow."

   c) "Volatility is fine if my long-term goals are met."

Reflection:

Mostly a's → Conservative: Prefer safety, lower growth.

Mostly b's → Balanced: Comfort with moderate risk.

Mostly C's → Aggressive: Can handle volatility for higher returns.

"Risk profile isn't permanent—it evolves with life stage, income, and goals."

Key Learnings:

- Don't invest based on fear or thrill—it's not a casino.
- Start with your goals and time horizon.
- Understand different types of risk—not just "market risk."
- Choose investments that offer better risk-adjusted returns.
- Review your risk profile periodically or when life changes.

"Risk is what's left over when you think you've thought of everything." – ***Carl Richards.***

Chapter 12

Comparing Asset Classes —And the Power of Asset Allocation

"Diversification is protection against ignorance."

— Warren Buffett

"Smart Investing starts with the right asset mix, not chasing the best fund". — ***The Economic Times***

When it comes to investing, most people are drawn to what's trending—gold in a crisis, real estate in a boom, or equity during a bull run.

But true wealth is built not by chasing returns, but by understanding risk and aligning assets with your goals.

There are 5 Main types of Asset Classes in India. They are:

1. **Fixed Income (Debt Instruments)**

- Average Return: ~6.5% to 7.5% p.a.
- Volatility: Low
- Example Instruments: PPF, Bank FDs, Debt MFs

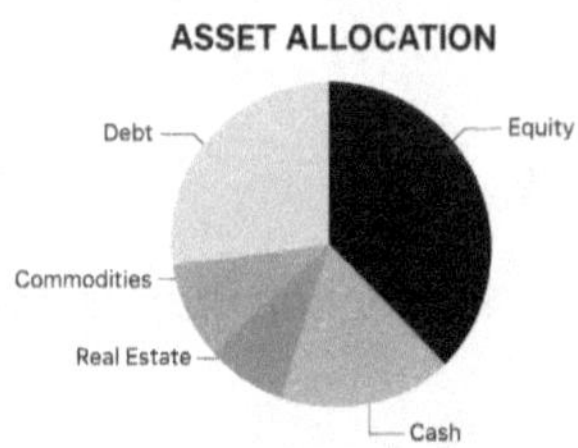

- Pros: Capital protection, stable income
- Cons: Low post-tax returns, may not beat inflation.

2. **Gold (Commodities)**

- Average Return: ~8.5% to 9.5% p.a.
- Volatility: Medium to High

- Key Insight: Gold surged during uncertainty but underperforms in stable or bullish equity markets.
- Role: Hedge against geopolitical and currency risk.

3. **Real Estate (India House Price Index - Residex)**

- Average Return: ~5% to 7% p.a. (excluding rental yield)
- Volatility: Low to Medium
- Issues: High transaction & maintenance costs, Low liquidity, Regulatory risks
- Real estate is more of a consumption asset than a wealth builder for most individuals.

4. **Equity (Nifty 500 TRI)**

- Average Return: ~12.5% to 14% p.a.
- Volatility: High (short-term); Low (long-term)
- Best Performing Asset (10-year CAGR)
- Insight: Short-term volatility scares many, but equity rewards the patient and the disciplined.

5. **Cash (Bank FDs, Liquid Funds)**

- Average Return: ~ 4% to 7%
- Volatility: Very Low
- Liquidity: High
- Safety: Very High
- Use: Ideal for Emergency Fund (3 to 6 Months of expenses)

Client Story: The Power of Asset Allocation

Sonal, a 38-year-old entrepreneur, had always invested based on instinct—putting most of her money into real estate and a few equity funds recommended by friends. While some years looked good, her wealth felt scattered and unpredictable.

When she consulted us, we introduced her — asset allocation—the simple but powerful principle of distributing investments across equity, debt, gold, and real estate based on her goals and risk appetite. Over time, this strategy transformed her financial life. Equity provided growth, debt gave stability, gold hedged against uncertainty, and real estate added long-term value.

During a market downturn, while her equity investments dipped, her debt and gold holdings cushioned the impact. Instead of panic, she felt calm and in control.

Sonal realised that wealth creation wasn't about picking the "best" asset but about finding the **right balance.**

"Asset allocation doesn't just grow your wealth—it protects your peace of mind."

Comparative Snapshot (2013–2023)

Asset Class	Avg. Annual Return	Volatility	Liquidity	Tax Efficiency
Fixed Income	6.5% – 7.5%	Low	High	Moderate
Gold (Physical)	8.5% – 9.5%	Medium	High	Moderate
Real Estate (Physical)	5% – 7%	Low-Med	Low	Low
Equity (Nifty 500 TRI)	12% – 14%	High	High	High (LTCG)

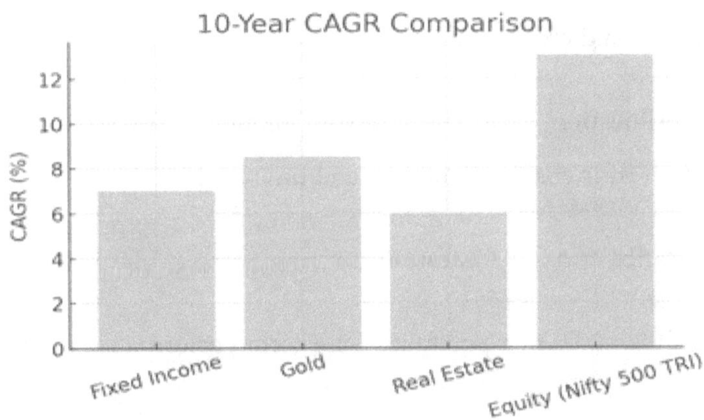

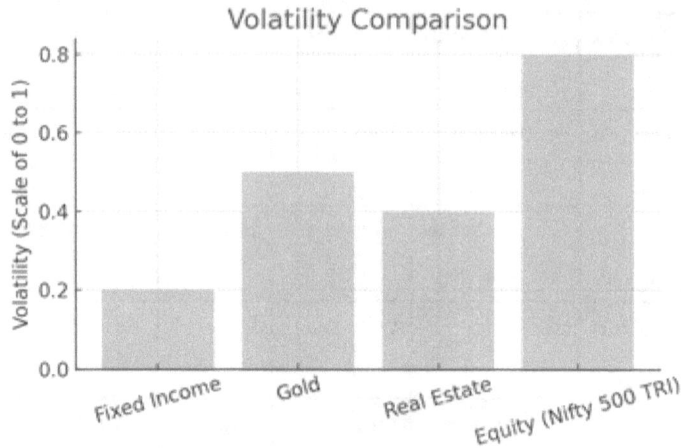

The Power of Asset Allocation

Imagine a cricket team with only batters or only bowlers. That's what a single-asset portfolio looks like. Balanced portfolios win matches—and create wealth.

Asset Allocation = Distributing your money across asset classes based on your goals, risk profile, and time horizon.

Importance of Asset Allocation

Around 85–90% of a portfolio's long-term performance is driven by asset allocation.

This comes from studies such as Brinson, Hood & Beebower (1986, 1991), which showed that the mix of assets (equity, debt, real estate, gold, etc.) matters far more than:

- Stock-picking
- Timing the market
- Choosing specific funds

"If you get your asset allocation right, you've already solved nearly 90% of the wealth-building equation."

Client Story: The Disciplined Investor vs. The Return Chaser

Ranjit and Nikita, colleagues in an IT firm with similar salaries, took very different investment paths.

Our client, Ranjit, invested in a disciplined manner (₹1 lakh per month). His SIPs were a balanced mix—60% equity, 30% debt, 10% gold—based on his top 3 goals. Nikita, on the other hand, kept chasing the next "hot" asset—real estate, then gold, now crypto.

Ten years later, Ranjit's portfolio had doubled with a 15% CAGR and peace of mind, while Nikita's money was stuck in volatile, illiquid bets, pushing her dream of early retirement further away. We trust Nikita will soon embrace discipline.

"Discipline builds wealth, chasing fads destroys it."

The Role of Debt Products in Asset Allocation

When we think of wealth creation, equity often steals the spotlight. Yet, no portfolio can be truly balanced without the quiet strength of debt products. Debt instruments — whether in the form of short-term debt funds, corporate deposits, bonds, or Non-Convertible Debentures (NCDs) — act as the stabilisers of asset allocation, ensuring that an investor's journey is steady and resilient.

Why Debt Matters

Debt products provide predictability, stability, and liquidity. Unlike equities, which can fluctuate sharply with market cycles, debt instruments generate fixed or relatively stable returns. This makes them essential for meeting short-term goals, maintaining emergency reserves, and cushioning against volatility.

- **Short-Term Debt Funds:** Ideal for parking surplus money, they offer higher returns than savings accounts with the benefit of liquidity.
- **Corporate Deposits:** Provide assured interest income, though selection requires due diligence on creditworthiness.
- **Bonds:** Government or high-grade corporate bonds add safety and steady income, balancing equity risk.
- **NCDs (Non-Convertible Debentures):** Offer attractive yields and are suitable for investors seeking predictable cash flows.

Strategic Role in Asset Allocation

By combining equities (for growth) with debt (for stability), investors achieve a risk-adjusted portfolio that not only compounds wealth but also protects capital during downturns. Debt allocation ensures you don't have to exit equities in panic during market corrections — instead, you have a safety cushion to rely on. For retirees, debt products become even more critical in generating regular income while preserving capital.

"Debt may not make headlines like equity, but in asset allocation, it is the unsung hero that protects, balances, and powers your wealth journey."

Client Story: Stability in Retirement

Mr Dilip Trivedi, a retired Manager from an Indian MNC, had always been conservative with money. While his children encouraged him to explore equities, he was more concerned about preserving capital and ensuring a steady monthly income.

Through a carefully designed asset allocation plan, we allocated a significant portion of his portfolio into short-term debt funds, bonds, and NCDs. These instruments provided him with regular interest payouts and liquidity, while a smaller allocation in equities kept his wealth growing.

Today, Mr Trivedi enjoys his retirement without financial stress —

his monthly income from debt products takes care of household expenses, while the equity portion is reserved for long-term growth and legacy.

"Debt products may not promise excitement, but they ensure peace of mind — the very foundation of a balanced and resilient portfolio."

Key Learnings:

- Don't pick favourites—pick a strategy.
- Volatility is your friend if you stay the course.
- Real wealth is built by discipline, diversification, and patience.
- Asset allocation is not a luxury—it's a necessity.
- Asset allocation is the most important investment decision.

Chapter 13

Money Mind Maps — Why and How to Create One?

"Clarity precedes success."

— Robin Sharma

Most people keep their financial information scattered—some in bank statements, some in investment account portals, and most in their heads.

The result? Missed payments, forgotten investments, and confusion about actual net worth.

A Money Mind Map changes all that. It helps you clarify your financial goals, track income and expenses, manage debt, and plan for the future.

What is a Money Mind Map?

A Money Mind Map is a visual diagram that shows your entire financial landscape in one place.

It's like Google Maps for your money—helping you see where you are, what's connected, and where you can go next.

Benefits of a Money Mind Map

- **Clarity at a Glance** — See your financial big picture instantly.
- **Better Decision Making** — Understand how new moves fit into your plan.
- **Identifying Gaps & Risks** — Spot weak areas before they become problems.

- **Goal Alignment** — Check if your habits match your goals.
- **Stress Reduction** — Reduce uncertainty and gain confidence.
- **Family Preparedness** — Make it easy for your family to access your financial roadmap.
- **Track Progress** — Visually track your goals, like paying off your debt
- **Simple Budgeting** — Move beyond numbers-based spreadsheets to a visual system.

How to Create Your Money Mind Map

1. **Choose Your Tool** — Pen & paper or popular free mind mapping Apps like XMind, Freeplane, or MindMeister.
2. **Start with YOU in the Centre** — This is your financial hub.
3. **Branch Out into Categories** — Income, Expenses, Assets, Liabilities, Goals, Protection.
4. **Add Sub-Branches** — For example, under Assets: Equity Funds, Debt Funds, Fixed Deposits, Gold, Property.
5. **Add Relevant Data** — Include account numbers, policy details, and renewal dates.
6. **Review & Update Regularly** — Adjust for new investments, paid-off loans, or updated goals.

Client Story: From Money Leaks to Money Goals

Ravindra, a mid-level IT manager, earned well but felt constant financial stress. He attended our Money Mind Map workshop in 2022 and thereafter created his own Money Mind Map. It revealed a hard truth —he was overspending 25% on dining and subscriptions.

By visualising his money flow and seeking our help, Ravindra redirected that leakage into a SIP—fast-tracking his retirement by 4 years.

"When you can see your money clearly, you can control it. When you control it, it works for you—not the other way around."

Pro Tips for a Powerful Money Mind Map

- **Colour Code** — Green for assets, red for liabilities, blue for goals.
- **Keep it Simple** — Avoid clutter; make it easy to read at a glance.
- **Secure it** — Store securely, whether digital or physical.
- **Share with Trusted Family** — Ensure they know where things stand.
- **Look at your Money Mind Map twice daily** — to harness the power of visualisation

Sample Money Mind Map Diagram

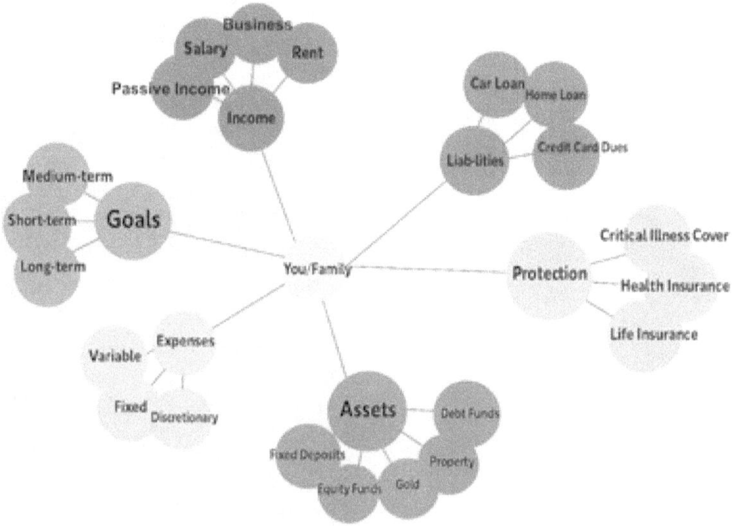

Your Turn: Create your Money Mind Map

ake a moment to sketch your **Money Mind Map** (on a blank page) — a visual snapshot of how you think, feel, and act about money today.

Add your real numbers to the Money Mind Map—it's the only way to truly understand where you stand financially.

My Money Mind Map

Chapter 14

Mutual Funds — The What, Which, Why, and How?

"The best time to plant a tree was 20 years ago. The second best time is now."

— Chinese Proverb

"Don't work for money. Make your money work for you." — ***Robert Kiyosaki***

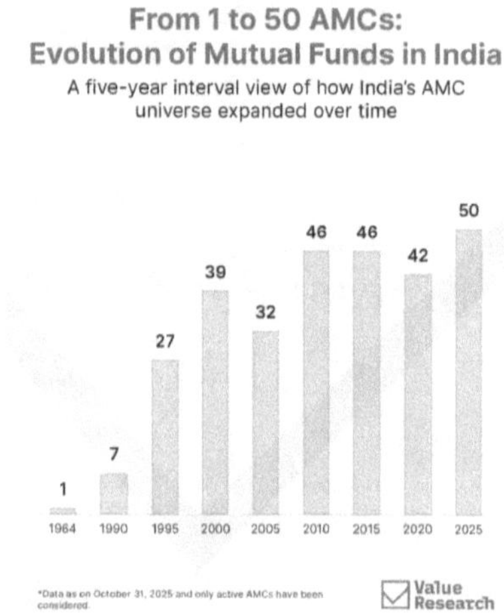

Mutual Funds have emerged as one of the most powerful investment tools for the modern Indian investor.

The Indian mutual fund industry is growing at around ~18–19% year-on-year, with AUM at approximately ₹80.8 lakh crore (₹80.8 trillion) as of November 2025, supported by a broadening investor base and strong inflows — and is serviced by around 50 AMCs.

Whether it's building wealth, funding your child's future, retiring early, or outpacing inflation, mutual funds provide a professional, diversified, and accessible way to reach your goals.

And yet, many are either overwhelmed by the options or misinformed by myths.

This chapter breaks it down — the why and the how of mutual funds.

What are Mutual Funds?

Think of a mutual fund like a group lunch. Instead of each person ordering and paying for a full meal alone, everyone pools some money, and the group enjoys a variety of dishes together. In the same way, investors pool their money into a mutual fund, which a professional fund manager uses to buy a mix of stocks, bonds, or gold.

This way, even with a small contribution, you get the benefit of variety, expert management, and shared growth.

"A mutual fund is simply many people pooling money to grow together, managed by an expert."

Why Invest in Mutual Funds?

Mutual funds offer many benefits, with the key ones being:

- **Diversification** – Your money is spread across a basket of securities, reducing unsystematic risk and achieving the desired asset allocation
- **Professional Management** – Fund managers actively monitor and optimise the portfolio
- **Liquidity** – Most open-ended funds can be redeemed anytime
- **Flexibility** – Start with as little as ₹100 via SIP, Pause or stop without any penalty.

- **Tax Efficiency** – The long-term (more than 1 year) Capital gains (≥ ₹1.25 Lakhs in a Financial year) on equity funds are taxed at only 12.5%
- **Accessibility** – Mobile Application to access the reports along with periodic statements
- **Transparency** – NAVs disclosed daily, detailed fact sheets, SEBI regulations
- **Customisation** – There's a fund for every goal and risk appetite
- **Disciplined Investments** – The mutual fund SIPs offer a disciplined approach towards investing with the flexibility of stop, pause, or step-up.

"Mutual funds offer diversification, professional management, and the power of compounding—all in one simple investment."

Which Mutual Fund Categories to Choose (and why)?

Here are the main mutual fund categories, their purpose, and where they fit best:

Category	Purpose	Ideal For
Equity Funds	Long-term wealth creation	Investors with a> 5-year horizon
Debt Funds	Stability, low-risk income	Conservative investors, short-term goals

Hybrid Funds	Balance between growth & safety	Moderate-risk investors
Index Funds/ ETFs	Passive exposure to markets	Cost-conscious, long-term investors
Multi-Asset Funds	Diversify across equity, debt, and gold	All-weather portfolios
Small Cap/ Mid Cap Funds	Higher growth potential	Aggressive investors with patience
Multi-Factor Funds	Rule-based smart beta strategy	Smart beta investors
Thematic/ Sectoral Funds	Focused bets like Pharma, Infra	Niche investors
ELSS (Tax Saving)	Save tax under 80C	Salaried, goal-based savers
Liquid/ Overnight Funds	Short-term parking is better than FD	Emergency corpus or idle cash

Matching Mutual Funds with Financial Goals

Here are the goal types and the matching mutual fund categories:

Financial Goal	Suggested Fund Category
Emergency Fund	Liquid/Overnight Fund
Child's Education	SIP in Equity Fund + Hybrid Fund
Buying a House (5–7 yrs)	Hybrid + Short Duration Debt Funds
Retirement (15+ yrs)	Equity Funds + Multi-Asset Funds
Tax Saving (u/s 80 C – Old Tax Regime)	**Retirement** Savings Fund with 5 years locking/ Equity Linked Saving Scheme
World Tour in 3 years	Short Duration + Balanced Advantage

SIP — The Wealth Multiplier

A Systematic Investment Plan (SIP) is not just convenient — it's a discipline enabler. You invest a fixed amount monthly, irrespective of market levels. Over time, this allows you to:

- Benefit from Rupee Cost Averaging
- Cultivate a habit of saving before spending
- Build wealth with less emotional interference

SIP Example:

Monthly SIP	Tenure	Returns @12% CAGR	Wealth Accumulated
₹5,000	10 years	₹11.6 lakhs	₹8 lakhs invested
₹10,000	20 years	₹76.5 lakhs	₹24 lakhs invested

Client Story: Steady Growth with Mutual Funds

Supriyo and Dipali Gupta were clueless about how to secure their future and achieve their goals. Unsure where to begin, they approached us for guidance in 2013. With a clear financial roadmap and a disciplined Goal-based SIP plan, they gained confidence and clarity. Over the years, their investments have grown steadily, helping them move closer to their family's goals and financial freedom.

Today, they look back with gratitude at the journey — the ease of investing through mutual funds, the power of compounding working silently in the background, and the assurance that their goals are well within reach.

As Dipali shared, *"The discipline of SIPs through Mutual Funds gave us peace of mind and confidence that our dreams are achievable."*

Step-Up/ Top-Up SIP — A Game Changer

If your salary increases annually, shouldn't your SIP?

With Step-Up SIP (also known as Top-Up SIP), you increase your investment amount each year by a fixed percentage or amount. This small tweak can lead to exponential growth.

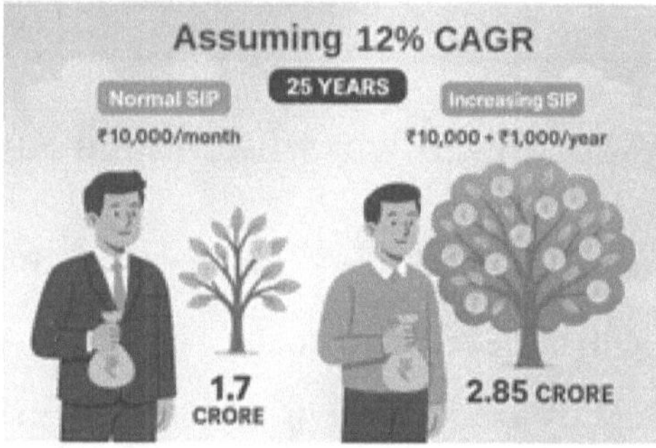

Client Story: The Power of Small Steps

When Arjun began his investment journey, he committed just ₹10,000 a month to SIPs. On our recommendation, he increased this amount by 10%—just ₹1,000 annually.

Over 10 years, this small discipline has created a big difference. With step-up SIPs, Arjun's wealth grew to **₹33 lakhs.** Without the step-up, it would have been only **₹22.50 Lakhs.**

That's an extra **₹10.5 Lakhs,** simply by letting compounding work on small, consistent increases.

"Wealth is built not by leaps, but by steady steps."

Common Mistakes to Avoid

- Comparing different mutual funds purely by past returns instead of risk-adjusted returns
- Redeeming the fund or stopping the SIPs prematurely in panic
- Chasing trending thematic funds without understanding risks
- Over-diversifying into too many funds
- Ignoring portfolio reviews and rebalancing
- Choosing the funds purely on past performance without checking if those suit your goals
- Failing to go through the scheme details or presentation to understand its risks and rewards
- Buying direct funds just to save costs, without knowledge

Mutual Funds Are Like Tailored Suits—Perfect Fit Matters

You don't buy the fanciest suit — you buy what fits. Similarly, choose mutual funds that fit your goals, risk appetite, and time horizon. And as your life changes, adjust your investment wardrobe accordingly.

Work with a trusted financial advisor or coach, stay consistent, and trust the power of compounding and discipline.

"Don't just cut costs—create value that counts."

Key Learnings:

- **One Size Doesn't Fit All** – Mutual funds should be chosen based on your financial goals, risk appetite, and investment horizon, not trends or friend recommendations.
- **Asset Allocation Matters** – Diversifying across equity, debt, and other fund types reduces risk and enhances long-term wealth creation.
- **Understand Risk vs. Return** – Higher returns come with higher risk; evaluate if the risk aligns with your comfort and financial plan.
- **Consistency Beats Timing** – Regular, disciplined investments through SIPs often outperform attempts to time the market.
- **Review and Rebalance** – Periodic reviews ensure your portfolio stays aligned with changing goals.

Chapter 15

Investing— Without Losing Sleep & Making Money While You Sleep

"If you don't find a way to make money while you sleep, you will work until you die."

— Warren Buffett

"Investing is simple — but not easy. It requires patience, purpose, and protection from noise."

If you've ever stayed awake worrying about markets, you're not alone.

This chapter will show you how to let your money work for you — so you can grow wealth, calmly and confidently.

Investing vs. Trading vs. Speculation — Know the Difference

Investing is long-term ownership. Trading is short-term buying and selling. Speculation is betting without research. True wealth is created by **staying invested**, not chasing market highs.

A simple ₹10,000 monthly SIP in the Nifty 50 for 15 years can grow to over ₹50 lakhs — proof that time in the market matters more than timing the market.

"Markets reward patience, not prediction."

SIP or Lump Sum — Choose What Fits You

Systematic Investment Plans (SIPs) build discipline and average **out volatility — ideal for salaried individuals with steady income.**

Lump sums, on the other hand, work well for bonuses, inheritances, or windfalls — best used in falling or sideways markets.

If you want to invest gradually, use a **Systematic Transfer Plan (STP)** — moving money from a low-risk debt fund to an equity or hybrid fund over time.

Even self-employed individuals can park surpluses in short-term debt funds and set up STPs to steadily build wealth toward long-term goals.

"SIP Karo, Mast Raho— Lumpsum Karo, Jab Surplus Ho!"

The PPF vs NPS Shift — From Safety to Smart Growth

Three decades ago, the Public Provident Fund (PPF) was a star performer — offering 11–12% guaranteed returns, tax benefits, and safety when few other options existed. Back then, inflation was lower, and a double-digit fixed return meant real wealth creation.

But over time, as India's economy matured, interest rates fell sharply — PPF today offers only 7.1% p.a, barely 1–2% above inflation. With minimal equity exposure and limited flexibility, it has become more of a capital preservation tool than a wealth creator.

In contrast, the National Pension System (NPS) offers market-linked growth, diversified asset allocation (equity + debt), and returns averaging 9–12% CAGR over the long term. It also provides extra tax deductions, making it far more efficient for retirement planning:

- Up to ₹50,000/- u/s 80CCD(1B) — available under the old tax regime for NPS Tier 1 account
- Employer contribution benefits u/s 80CCD (2) — Up to 14% of your salary (basic dearness allowance) under both old and new tax regimes.

While NPS carries some market risk, its ability to beat inflation, build a larger corpus, and create sustainable post-retirement income makes it a superior choice for long-term investors today — a shift from safety to smart growth.

"What worked yesterday may not work tomorrow—especially in finance."

The Power of Asset Allocation

"Don't put all your eggs in one basket — put purpose in every basket."

A diversified portfolio outperforms random fund picking, offering steadier returns and lower volatility by combining assets with a strong inverse correlation — meaning they tend to move in opposite directions under similar market conditions—are crucial for enhancing portfolio stability through diversification.

For example, a 60:30:10 split between **Equity, Debt, Gold** and brings both growth and stability.

- Equity for growth
- Debt for stability
- Gold for protection

"The goal isn't to find the "best" fund — it's to build the right basket."

Can Hybrid Funds Beat the Small Cap Index or the Nifty 500?

The Surprising Truth About Asset Allocation

Many investors assume that only high-equity portfolios can create long-term wealth. But history shows something far more powerful:

Hybrid funds with less than 65% equity—when backed by smart asset allocation—have often delivered equity-like returns with far lower volatility.

In several market cycles, dynamic and aggressive hybrid funds have even outperformed both the Small Cap Index and the Nifty

500 TRI, not by taking more risk, but by allocating risk better.

Funds	3 Months (Absolute %)	1 Year (CAGR %)	3 Years (CAGR %)	5 Years (CAGR %)	10 Years (CAGR %)
ICICI Prudential Equity & Debt Fund	4.51	12.52	18.99	24.02	16.21
ICICI Prudential Multi Asset Fund	6.57	15.06	18.94	23.53	16.1
ICICI Prudential Balanced Advantage Fund	3.91	11.51	13.53	13.56	11.41
ICICI Prudential Dynamic Asset Allocation Active FoF	2.12	9.46	13.89	14.29	12.58
Nifty Smallcap 250 Index	-3.52	-4.46	20.05	24.5	N.A.
Nifty Midcap 150 Index	6.19	8	23.5	24.6	17.5
Nifty 500 Index	5.19	6.2	15.1	17.4	13.6

(Performance as on 26 November 2025)

Why does this happen?

- Rebalancing discipline: profits booked automatically, losses limited.
- Built-in asset allocation: equity + debt + cash cushions during crashes.
- Lower drawdowns: protects compounding during bad years.
- Volatility efficiency: smoother journey, fewer behavioural mistakes.

The Big Lesson

- You don't always need more equity to create more wealth.
- You need the right mix, at the right time, with the right discipline.

"Asset allocation is not about chasing returns — it's about controlling risk so that returns can chase you."

Index vs Active Funds — Why Companies Create Wealth, Not Markets

There is a simple truth hidden beneath years of market noise:

"Markets don't create wealth. Companies do."

Over the last 15 years, data from India's top 500 companies reveals a powerful pattern:

Every single year, 100–350 companies delivered more than 15% CAGR over rolling 5-year periods. These are the real compounders — the engines of long-term wealth creation. An index simply averages them out.

But an actively managed fund captures more of these winners and avoids the laggards — and this is where alpha is born.

Why Index Funds Matter

Index funds are low-cost, relatively more stable, and ideal for broad market exposure. They give you the market's return — nothing more, nothing less.

Where Actively Managed Funds Win

Great fund managers don't buy the whole market. They handpick:

- High-quality businesses
- Scalable models

- Strong balance sheets
- Consistent earnings compounders
- And they avoid companies that destroy value.

This ability to own more of the right companies is what has historically delivered 2–5% alpha over benchmarks in India — a difference that becomes massive when compounded over 10–15 years.

The Real Lesson

India is a fast-growing, high-dispersion market. Not all companies move together. But a select few consistently outperform — and identifying them creates real wealth. So don't chase the market.

Choose funds that choose the right companies.

"Alpha is generated when you consistently back the top 20% compounders and avoid the bottom 20% destroyers."

Direct vs. Regular Mutual Funds — The Hidden Cost of 'Zero Commission'

"Why pay a commission? It will eat into my SIP returns!"

That's the most common argument online. On paper, it sounds convincing.

Example:

- ₹30,000 SIP in **Direct Funds** at 12% for 35 years = ₹20.8 crores
- ₹30,000 SIP in **Regular Funds** at 11% (after 1% commission) = ₹15.9 crores
- *Difference = ₹4.9 crores!*

Scary? Yes — until you see what actually happens in real life.

DIY Investing — The Reality Check

"Zero commission" often comes with hidden costs — stress, confusion, and missed opportunities.

Common pitfalls include:

- Overwhelm from 2,500+ fund choices
- Chasing last year's top performers
- Panic selling during market crashes
- Jumping into "hot" sectors at the wrong time

As a result, most DIY investors earn barely **8–9%,** instead of the assumed 12%.

That same ₹30,000 SIP at 9% grows to ₹11.4 crores — **₹9.4 crores less** than expected and **₹5.5 crores less** than advised investors who pay up to 1% extra (higher expense ratio) for the regular funds.

Advised Investing — Pay Less Attention, Earn More

A guided investor using **Regular Plans** benefits from:

- Smart fund selection
- Strategic asset allocation
- Discipline through market cycles
- Periodic reviews and rebalancing

That 1% "cost" buys peace of mind — and up 5% better returns.

"The real cost isn't the fee you pay — it's the mistakes you make without advice."

Client Story: From Dreams to Reality

Pallavi and Santosh Bhise, IT professionals, realised during the pandemic that disciplined savings and DIY investing weren't enough.

With a clear roadmap and coaching, they aligned investments with their goals — and soon fulfilled their dream of a family trip to Europe.

Now, their money and mindset are both in balance — and they are now confidently walking the path to financial freedom.

"Clarity turns savings into milestones — and dreams into reality."

Beyond Mutual Funds — Investing for the Affluent

Once your financial foundation is strong, you can explore advanced strategies such as **PMS, AIFs, and MLDs.** These vehicles are for investors with larger portfolios and a higher appetite for managed risk — offering professional expertise and access to niche opportunities.

PMS & AIFs — Tailored Wealth for the Affluent

Portfolio Management Services (PMS) create personalised equity or debt portfolios, while

Alternative Investment Funds (AIFs) pool money into specialised strategies like private equity, venture capital, or structured debt.

Minimum investment: ₹50 lakhs (PMS) or ₹1 crore (AIF).

Pros:

- Professional management and diversification
- Access to unlisted and thematic opportunities
- Customisation and detailed reporting

Cons:

- Higher costs and risks
- Less liquidity
- Manager performance varies

These are best for **HNIs and NRIs** who've secured their core goals and want to explore higher-return avenues.

Client Story: The Diversification Edge

The Patel family from Mumbai already had bank NCDs, Fixed Deposits, Large-cap and hybrid Mutual funds, and real estate in their investment portfolio. They wanted diversification and a slightly higher return— and hence allocated a portion of their Fixed Deposits to a high-conviction PMS in 2023.

While their mutual funds compounded steadily, the ICICI Prudential PMS- Pipe Strategy added alpha (CAGR ~ 32%) from the mid and small cap segments. This combination strengthened their portfolio — and their confidence.

"PMS and AIFs can be powerful wealth creators — but only for HNI investors who combine capital with patience."

Beyond Mutual Funds — For Retail Investors

1) Market-Linked Debentures (MLDs) — Growth with Protection

For investors seeking a balance between safety and returns, MLDs offer structured solutions — linking returns to market performance (like gold or equity indices), while providing downside protection.

Example — The Gold Twin Win by Nuvama Wealth:

- Underlying: MCX Gold Mini
- Return: Minimum 4% p.a. or actual gold returns, whichever is higher
- Tenure: 42 months

If gold underperforms, you still earn 4%. If it shines, you share in the upside.

Why More Investors Are Turning to MLDs:

- Capital protection with growth potential
- Predictable timelines
- Exposure to varied asset classes
- Low stress, low maintenance

"MLDs aren't for chasing markets — they're for structuring peace of mind."

2) REITs & InViTs — Fractional Ownership, Full Potential

Real estate and infrastructure are no longer the playgrounds of the wealthy.

REITs (Real Estate Investment Trusts) and **InViTs** (Infrastructure Investment Trusts) allow you to participate in income-generating assets with as little as ₹10,000.

You earn through quarterly distributions (like rent) and potential capital gains — minus the hassle of maintenance or tenants.

Benefits:

- Low entry point
- Regular income streams
- Portfolio diversification
- Liquidity and transparency
- SEBI-regulated structure

"REITs and InViTs let you own a piece of India's growth — without owning the headache."

Client Story: Priya's Peace of Mind

Priya, 36, an HR professional from Pune, longed to own commercial property but found it unaffordable. Through REITs, she started small — ₹50,000 — and began receiving quarterly payouts.

Later, she diversified into an InViT linked to toll roads and transmission lines, earning stable returns (~12.5% CAGR).

"Fractional investing helped me live my dream — income, growth, and peace of mind, without large capital."

Should You Go Global?

Yes — but only as a satellite allocation.

Global funds can add diversification and access to world-class innovators like Apple, and Tesla, but they should complement — not replace — your core India-focused portfolio, where long-term growth potential is far stronger.

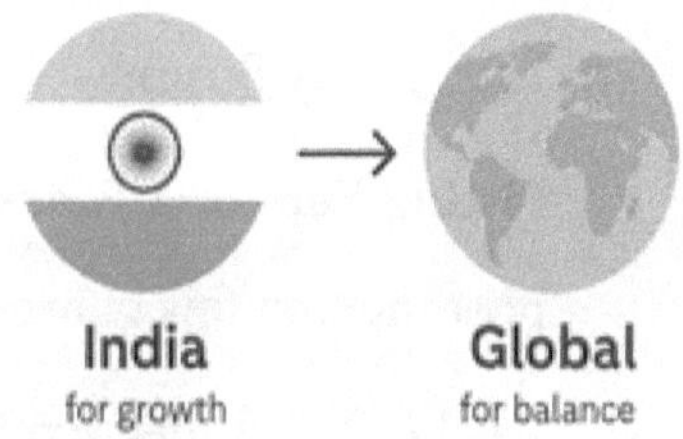

At Adyanta, we recommend 5–15% global exposure for mature investors with a strong India core who want diversification, USD exposure, and access to the.mes like AI, biotech, semiconductors, and global leaders.

Think of it as: **"India for growth, global for balance."**

Should You Invest in an IPO?

IPO season often brings excitement — glossy ads, celebrity endorsements, and promises of the "next big thing."

But beneath the glamour lies a crucial truth: **IPOs are a seller's market, while the secondary market is where prices are truly discovered.**

As an investor, patience often outperforms enthusiasm. Great companies don't become great because of their debut day; they prove themselves over time through performance, governance, and delivery.

Before Investing in an IPO, Remember:

- **IPO ≠ Bargain:** The seller (company) decides the price, not the market.
- **Prospectus is a Pitch:** Real performance begins after listing. Buy Businesses, Not Brochures.
- **Listing Euphoria Fades:** Watch how the business adjusts post the first few quarters.
- **Anchor Lock-ins Expire:** Supply often increases later, affecting prices.
- **Promises vs. Delivery:** Focus on what management does, not what it plans.
- **Promoter Dilution = Red Flag:** Seasoned investors prefer "skin in the game."
- **Oversubscription ≠ Outperformance:** Hype doesn't guarantee returns — discipline does.
- **Patience pays:** It's wiser to buy after reality reveals itself than to chase stories untested by time.

"Let time test the business — not your greed. Because in investing, discovery always beats hype."

GOLD or SILVER ETF — Which and How Much Should you invest in?

Precious metals have once again captured India's imagination.

With Gold ETFs delivering over 65% returns in the last year and Silver ETFs rallying 75–85%, many investors are asking a common question:

"Which one is better — Gold or Silver?"

The answer lies in understanding the role each metal plays in your financial life.

GOLD: The Protector of Wealth

Gold's rally over the past year has been driven by:

- Rising geopolitical uncertainties
- US recession fears
- Rate-cut expectations
- Record central bank purchases
- Weakening global currencies

Gold is not meant to generate high returns year after year. Its deeper purpose is risk reduction.

Gold is the seatbelt of your portfolio — not the engine. It stabilises your long-term wealth by reducing volatility, protecting purchasing power, and balancing equity-heavy portfolios.

A sensible allocation: 5–10% (up to 15% for conservative investors).

SILVER: The Accelerator of Growth

Silver has outperformed gold significantly in the last year with 75–85% returns — thanks to a powerful combination of industrial and investment demand.

Key drivers:

- Massive adoption of solar panels
- Heavy usage in electric vehicles (EVs)
- Growth in semiconductors and electronics
- Global clean-energy transition
- A persistent supply deficit for the third consecutive year

Silver is no longer just a precious metal — it is becoming the metal of the future.

But there's a catch:

Silver is extremely volatile. Historically, it has corrected 30–50% multiple times, and the 2011 crash wiped out nearly 60%.

Silver can boost your returns — or shake your peace — depending on how you use it.

A prudent allocation: 2–5% for moderately aggressive investors.

Remember: Do not invest in gold or silver because they have gone up.

- Invest because your portfolio needs balance, protection, or growth.
- If you want stability, choose Gold.
- If you want a higher but riskier return potential, choose Silver.
- If you want a smart, diversified portfolio, hold both — in the right proportion.

GOLD vs SILVER

FEATURE		
1-YEAR RETURN	~ 65%	75-85%
VOLATILITY	Low	Very high
ROLE	Risk reducer	Return enhancer
INDUSTRIAL USE	Limited	Very high (solar, EV, chips)
IDEAL ALLOCATION	5-10%	2-5%
BEST FOR	All investors	Aggressive investors

(As of 10th Nov. 2025)

The key is discipline, not excitement.

"Precious metals don't reward impulse. They reward intelligent allocation."

Client Story: From Confusion to Clarity

Sagar Bhagwat, Assistant Manager at TCS, was anxious about his scattered investments. With our guidance, he aligned his portfolio to life goals and stopped reacting to market noise.

Today, he invests with clarity and calm, and yet has a portfolio CAGR of 14%+.

"True wealth isn't just about returns — it's about sleeping peacefully knowing your money is in the right place."

The Smart Way to Choose Between Investment Options

Choosing between investment options becomes simpler when you follow a clear decision framework. Start with your goals — what you want the money to achieve and when you'll need it. Match each goal with the right time horizon, risk level, and expected return. Then evaluate products through a simple lens: **Safety, Liquidity, Returns, Costs, and Tax Efficiency.**

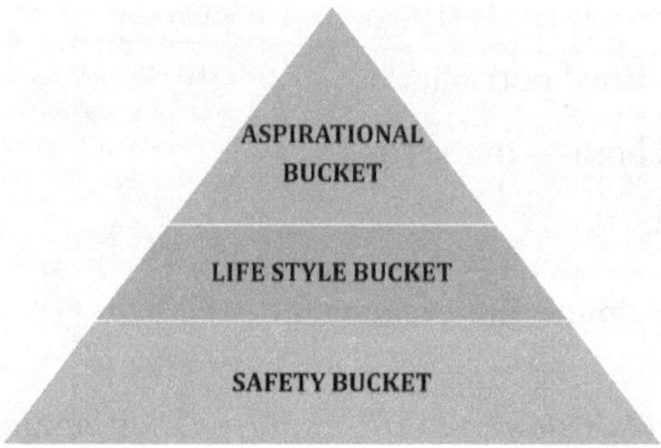

Your product selection must always begin from the bottom of the pyramid — first secure your Safety Bucket (Emergency Fund, Term Insurance, Health Insurance), then strengthen your Lifestyle Bucket (Balanced Funds, Multi-Asset Funds), and only after that allocate to the Aspirational Bucket (Small Caps, Thematic Funds, PMS, AIF).

When your foundation is strong, your aspirations can grow without fear — a family with a 6-month emergency corpus and adequate protection is far better positioned to invest confidently in opportunities like Small Cap Funds or International ETFs.

"When your investment choice aligns with your goals, risk appetite, and these core parameters, you're not just picking a product — you're building a strategy that works for you."

Adyanta Financials' Investment Selection Framework

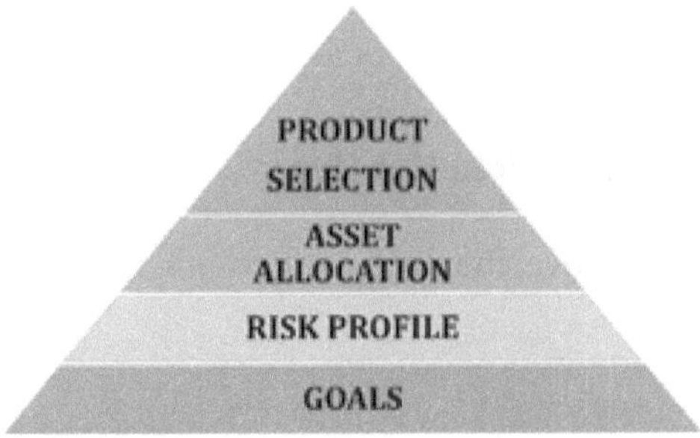

To ensure the best-fit investments for our clients, we follow a rigorous 16-point framework, detailed below:

1. Goals First, Products Later

Every investment must map to a life goal — education, home, retirement, or freedom.

2. Risk Profiling Before Returns

We evaluate risk tolerance, risk capacity, and time horizon — the real driver of outcomes.

3. Wealth Needs Discipline, Not Drama

Long-term consistency always beats shortcuts and excitement.

4. No F&O for Retail Investors

It destroys behaviour, promotes speculation, and breaks discipline.

5. No Crypto Until Regulations Mature

Without strong fundamentals and clarity, it stays outside core portfolios.

6. IPOs Require Validation, Not Hype

Businesses must prove themselves through market cycles before inclusion.

7. Asset Allocation > Asset Selection

Deciding how much in each asset class matters more than which fund.

8. Process + Allocation + Review > Emotion

Structured processes beat noise, opinions, and impulsive decisions.

9. Slow & Steady Compounding Wins

A portfolio with 12% disciplined compounding outperforms "fast money" traps.

10. Risk First, Returns Later

Protect capital and manage drawdowns — longevity improves compounding.

11. Stay Within Circle of Competence

Choose simple, understandable instruments — avoid unnecessary complexity.

12. Behaviour Management Is Wealth Management

Avoid panic-selling, greed-led buying, and recency bias.

13. Data-Led Fund Selection

We screen funds on 14 parameters such as consistency, portfolio quality, risk-adjusted returns, and manager philosophy.

14. Periodic Review & Rebalancing

Markets change. Life changes. Portfolios must be realigned regularly.

15. Protect the Foundation

Term insurance, health insurance, and an emergency fund are non-negotiable.

16. Taxes, Liquidity & Cash Flow Matter

True wealth is not just high returns — it's having money available when needed.

"We don't chase returns — we design disciplined, goal-aligned wealth."

Key Learnings

- Use a clear decision framework to select the right investment products.
- Review performance annually, not daily, and filter out social media noise.
- Avoid DIY overload — seek a coach, advisor, or planner.
- SIPs + Asset Allocation = Peaceful Compounding.
- Explore PMS/AIFs only after building your foundation.

"Investing without losing sleep isn't about timing the market — it's about trusting your plan, staying consistent, and letting time and discipline do their quiet magic."

Chapter 16

Invest Like a Pro — With Your Goals at the Centre

"The goal isn't more money. The goal is living life on your terms."

— Chris Brogan

"Most people plan their vacations better than they plan their life's biggest financial milestones."

Every Indian family wants to provide the best for their children — a quality education, a comfortable home, and a peaceful retirement. Yet, in the pursuit of one goal, many unknowingly push another to the sidelines.

True financial wisdom is about harmony — not how much we give, but how well we balance. With clarity, discipline, and a sound financial plan, you can turn multiple dreams into reality — theirs and yours. This chapter reveals how to achieve multiple financial goals with clarity and precision.

Why Goals Should Drive Your Money

People chase returns, trends, and news. But wealth is built when money has a purpose.

A parent investing ₹15K/month in equity mutual funds for 10

years for their child's higher education stays calm in market dips. Why? Because they know the goal.

"A financial goal provides direction and purpose to your money."

Planning for Higher Education

- Start early — preferably when the child is less than a year old.
- Cost inflation— ₹25 Lakhs today~, ₹ 1 Crore in 15 years (assuming 10% inflation)
- Use equity mutual funds for long-term corpus (10+ years)
- Use SIP + Step-up SIP. Start small and increase by 10 - 15% annually.
- Plan early for your child's professional degree—aligned to their talent, dreams, and your budget, even if not everything is clear today.

"A child's education is like a canvas, where every lesson adds a stroke of brilliance."

Client Story: From New Parents to Pro Investors

When Siddharth and Gandhali Bhagwat, both architects, became parents, their priorities shifted overnight. They wanted to give their newborn son the best possible education and a secure future — but like most young parents, they weren't sure where to begin.

That's when they approached us for financial coaching. Together, we created a roadmap that aligned their dreams — funding their son's higher education, buying a home in Powai, and starting their own practice.

Fast forward 4 years: With disciplined investing, smart asset allocation, and periodic reviews, they have already achieved their dream home, steadily building the corpus for their child's education, and are on their way to realising financial freedom much before their retirement.

"When dreams meet direction, Financial Freedom becomes inevitable."

Buying Your Dream Home — Emotion vs Logic

- Owning a house is emotional. But it must be affordable and well-timed.
- Invest for the 20% down payment first and take a home loan for the balance 80%.
- **Our Thumb rule:** EMI should not exceed 30 % of your take-home income.
- Consider a second home only after key goals are secured—and not as an investment.
- Choose REITs/InvITs over property —they offer better returns, more liquidity, and lower investment amounts.

- Buy a home only if you plan to stay 7+ years in the property.

"Home is where warmth whispers, memories echo, and stories unfold."

Client Story: From Anxiety to Achievement

In 2020, my friend Meruna Das, an HR professional, and her husband Rabindra approached me for financial coaching.

They were anxious about their future, unsure how to balance multiple goals. Together, we built a clear financial roadmap, and they followed it with discipline.

The result? Within the planned timeframe, they bought their dream home—comfortably within budget—without compromising on other goals.

With clarity and guidance, their anxiety turned into confidence, and their dream turned into reality.

"A well-crafted financial plan helps you achieve big goals without derailing the rest of your journey."

Before You Leap: Financial Planning for Entrepreneurs

Many professionals dream of leaving their jobs to start their entrepreneurial journey. But jumping without financial preparation is one of the costliest mistakes you can make.

Entrepreneurship is not just about passion — it demands patience, planning, and a strong safety net. Before you take the plunge, prepare yourself with these essentials:

- **Build Your Safety Net** —Save at least 12–18 months of essential expenses (rent, groceries, EMIs, insurance, school fees, and other non-negotiables). This cushion lets you survive without income while you build your venture.
- **Validate Your Idea First** — Test your idea as a side hustle. Get real customers, honest feedback, and proof of demand before you rely on it for a full-time income.
- **Know What You're Giving Up** — Quitting a job means losing more than salary — you also forgo health insurance, Provident Fund contributions, annual bonuses, and salary increments. Your business must replace all of these, not just your paycheck.
- **Be Realistic in Projections** — Cut your optimistic business numbers by half, and add six months to your expected timeline. Most businesses take 2–3 years to generate stable income.
- **Build the Right Support System** — Surround yourself with mentors, peers, and a trusted financial advisor. Their guidance, accountability, and encouragement will help you stay grounded and focused when challenges arise.

Quit your job only when you can afford to fail — financially, emotionally, and mentally. That's when you'll have the freedom to focus on building, not just surviving.

Client Story: The Power of Planning Before the Leap

Umesh Singh, a Banking and FinCrime Specialist, always dreamed of becoming an entrepreneur. Before taking the plunge, he approached us in 2018 to evaluate his finances and chart a roadmap for his start-up journey.

When we mapped his investments to key life goals — his son Aryan's higher education, a bigger home, and a secure retirement — the gap analysis revealed that patience would serve him better than haste. We advised him to first strengthen his short- and medium-term goals to ensure a smooth transition into entrepreneurship.

Today, Umesh has upgraded his home and funded Aryan's engineering education — entirely debt-free. With solid financial stability and valuable experience as a director in a Unicorn, he's now preparing to launch his venture in the next two years — on his own terms and timeline.

"With the right plan, dreams of entrepreneurship can grow without compromising life goals."

Retirement — The Longest Holiday of Your Life

You retire from work, not from expenses. Retirement, therefore, is the longest goal of your life as you need to plan for 25–30 years of post-retirement life. With longer lives, shorter careers, and changing family support, early retirement planning is essential.

Retirement planning isn't about age—it's about readiness. The sooner you start, the more freedom compounding gives you to build a secure future. Think beyond just savings; factor in inflation, rising healthcare costs, and the lifestyle you aspire to live.

A well-structured retirement plan ensures that your money works for you long after you stop active working, allowing you to enjoy your golden years with dignity, independence, and peace of mind, just like an extended dream vacation.

Adyanta's Golden Rule: 10:10:30 for Happy Retirement

If you're 30 or less — Commit just 10% of your combined family income towards Retirement SIPs, increase it by 10% each year, and let it grow at an estimated 15% CAGR over 30 years.

This simple habit can build a retirement corpus that safeguards your lifestyle, outpaces inflation, and sustains you for life.

"Retirement isn't an age. It's a funded lifestyle."

Beyond the "Proud Parent Syndrome"

Every year, countless Indian parents proudly sacrifice their comfort, hobbies, and dreams to fund their child's education abroad — believing they're giving them a better future.

But often, the price they pay goes far beyond money.

Take the story of the Patils from Pune. For over two decades, they lived frugally, saving every rupee for their son's U.S. education — ₹25–30 lakh on schooling and coaching, and over ₹1 crore for college abroad.

Today, their son is settled in New York, successful yet distant. The video calls are cheerful, but the silence afterwards is heavy. Their life savings are gone, and their emotional savings too — drained by loneliness.

This is the growing reality of #PICA — Parents Isolated, Children Away, a silent emotional and financial crisis in many Indian homes.

According to RBI data, India spends ₹1.5 lakh crore annually on overseas education — often by dipping into provident funds, retirement savings, or loans.

In the pursuit of securing their child's future, many parents unknowingly mortgage their own.

Yes, education is an investment — but it must not come at the cost of your peace, health, and financial dignity.

A sound financial plan balances love with logic — ensuring your child's dreams take flight without grounding your own stability.

Because true financial freedom isn't when your child succeeds abroad — it's when both generations thrive, independently and joyfully.

"In the race to give our children wings, let's not forget to keep our own roots nourished."

Asset Allocation and Product Strategy

Asset allocation is the foundation of a strong financial plan—it balances growth and stability based on your risk tolerance and goal horizon.

For medium-term goals (3–5 years), multi-asset funds offer the right mix of equity, debt, and gold. Those with lower risk appetite can also choose balanced advantage or multi-asset funds for steady progress toward long-term goals.

If your horizon exceeds 10 years and you can take a higher risk, begin with 100% equity and gradually reduce exposure over time—a progressive allocation strategy.

Products for Long-Term Goals

1. **Mutual Funds** (Equity and Hybrid Funds) - Flexible, liquid, and rewarding over time.
2. **Low-Cost ULIPs** - With annual premiums up to ₹2.5 lakh (within 10% of the sum assured), they offer investment, protection, and tax-free maturity under Section 10(10D).

For **retirement,** the **National Pension System** (NPS) can also be considered—**low-cost, tax-efficient, and flexible:**

- **Tier I:** Up to 75% equity
- **Tier II**: Up to 100% equity

"Step-up SIPs in Mutual Funds, Top-ups in ULIPs, or Tier-II NPS investments don't just grow your wealth—they turn your financial dreams into a peaceful, purposeful reality."

Common Planning Mistakes

1. Using the same fund or a common investment pool to chase multiple goals.
2. Investing without knowing how much is enough
3. Ignoring inflation in planning
4. Overloading real estate and underinvesting in liquid assets
5. Not allocating enough in equities for long-term goals

"A ₹50,000 lifestyle today will cost ₹2 lakh in 30 years at 8% inflation—plan early and let compounding secure your retirement."

Client Story: From Blind Spots to Bright Future

When 53-year-old Manoj Ratnaparkhe met us during a TCS helpdesk session, he had been investing diligently for his top 2 goals, namely — stress-free Retirement and Son's Higher education, but without direction.

A structured review revealed gaps — low-return traditional plans, no term or health cover, and minimal equity exposure.

We restructured his portfolio, balancing protection and growth. Manoj followed the plan with discipline, and today, he enjoys a **peaceful retirement** while his son Sanchit, now married, is well-settled in Canada after completing his master's there.

"Right strategy, and wise guidance accelerate your goals—and bring lasting peace of mind."

Your 5-Step Goal Planning Checklist

1. List your top 3 to 5 goals — timeline + target amount.
2. Start separate SIPs for each goal (name them!).
3. Use online calculators to estimate inflation-adjusted corpus.
4. Review every 12 months and adjust SIP if needed.
5. Don't pause SIPs in market falls — automate and stay consistent.

Top 5 Learnings

1. **Goal-based planning** removes panic and adds purpose.
2. **Start early** — especially for a child's education and retirement.
3. **Separate goals** = separate investments.
4. **Buy a house**, only when you're financially ready.
5. **Retirement planning** = Income replacement, not just saving.

Chapter 17

Revisit. Realign. Rebalance. — The Art of Periodic Reviews

"What gets measured gets improved."

— Peter Drucker

*"Planning is essential, but plans are useless if not reviewed." - **Adapted from Dwight D. Eisenhower.***

Life changes. So should your financial plan. Promotions, childbirth, relocation, inheritance, job loss — all these impact your goals, risk appetite, and cash flows.

Also, over a period of time:

- Products change
- Ratings change
- Markets change
- But the framework stays constant

Reviews are not just for returns — they're for relevance.

Review and Rebalancing: Keeping Your Portfolio on Track

Investing is not a "set it and forget it" exercise.

Even the best-designed portfolio can drift off-course due to market movements, changing goals, or life events.

That's where **review and rebalancing** come in—ensuring your investments stay aligned with your objectives.

What Should You Review?

1. Investment Portfolio:

- Is your asset allocation still aligned?
- Are your investments meeting expectations?
- Any laggards or underperformers?

2. Cash Flows:

- Has income increased? Are your expenses in check?
- Can you increase your SIPs or reduce EMIs?

3. Insurance & Protection:

- Are your term and health covers adequate?
- Are nominations updated?

4. Goals:

- Have your priorities shifted?
- Need to add a new goal? Modify timelines or amounts?

How to Review and Rebalance Effectively

You can review and rebalance your portfolio effectively simply by following our 5-step Framework:

1. **Set a schedule:** Review your portfolio at least once a year (half-yearly for goal-based plans and quarterly for actively managed portfolios).

2. **Revisit goals:** Check if your financial goals, timelines, or risk appetite have changed.
3. **Check allocation drift:** If equity or debt weightages have shifted significantly, rebalance to restore the original mix.
4. **Evaluate performance:** Compare fund/asset performance not just to returns, but also to benchmarks and your goals.
5. **Book profits wisely:** Move gains from volatile assets to stable ones as you near your goal.

How a Coach Can Help

A financial coach brings clarity and discipline.

He/she can:

- Spot risks and biases an investor may overlook.
- Recommend when to rebalance—without being swayed by emotions.
- Ensure reviews stay goal-based, not market-driven.
- Provide a structured framework for decision-making and enhance portfolio returns.
- Save precious time and effort, along with peace of mind.

Client Story – The Power of Regular Reviews

Ryan and Linuscia Pinto began their financial journey with Adyanta Financials in 2019. What set them apart was their commitment to regular reviews — treating them not as routine check-ins but as powerful tools for course correction.

Through these reviews, they upgraded insurances, rebalanced investments, and managed cash flows with clarity. Even amid market volatility and life's unpredictability, they stayed disciplined and focused on their goals.

Their journey proves a simple truth:

"A plan works best when it's reviewed, refined, and realigned regularly.

Key Benefits of Regular Review & Rebalancing

- **Protects gains** by moving profits into safer assets. For eg, if equity swells from 60% to 75% in a bull run, rebalancing realigns your portfolio and locks in gains
- **Reduces risk** cut risks by trimming weak assets and avoiding overexposure.
- **Keeps goals on track** despite market ups and downs.
- **Enhances Returns** by keeping your portfolio aligned and capturing new opportunities.

- **Adds peace of mind** knowing your portfolio is being monitored and adjusted.

"Markets will always move, but with review and rebalancing, your goals don't have to."

Client Story: The Cost of a Missed Review

Anita and Raj had a clear goal—building a corpus of ₹25 Lakhs for their daughter's higher education by 2022. Thanks to strong equity returns in the early years, they were well on track. But feeling confident, they skipped periodic reviews and let the portfolio run on autopilot.

When the markets crashed in 2020, their corpus suddenly dropped to ₹18 Lakhs. Had they conducted a structured annual review, part of the equity gains could have been shifted to safer debt instruments, protecting their progress.

That missed review didn't just cost them ₹5 Lakhs—it set their goal back by nearly three years of effort.

"The goal isn't to be perfect. The goal is to keep moving toward your destination, with timely course correction."

Key Learnings:

- **Review is Non-Negotiable** – Even the best portfolio needs regular check-ins to stay aligned with your life goals.

- **Goals Evolve, So Should Your Portfolio** – Marriage, children, career changes, or retirement milestones may demand realignment of investments.
- **Rebalancing Protects Gains** – Moving profits from volatile assets (like equity) into safer ones (like debt) safeguards progress.
- **Reduce Risk of Drift** – Market movements can tilt your asset allocation; rebalancing restores balance and prevents overexposure.
- **A Coach Adds Objectivity** – Professional guidance helps cut through biases and ensures timely, goal-based action.

Chapter 18

India Rising— Why NRIs, OCIs & PIOs are Increasingly Investing in India?

"The future depends on what you do today."

— Mahatma Gandhi

"If you're bullish on India, invest in India as a wealth builder."

Understanding why India is not just an Emerging Economy, but a market to invest in for long-term wealth creation, even for the Non-Resident Indians, Overseas Citizens of India, or Persons of Indian Origin.

This chapter unpacks why India's long-term economic story makes it a compelling equity destination.

India's Economic Momentum

- **Fastest growing major economy**: India's GDP is projected to grow over 6% annually for the next decade—outpacing developed economies and even emerging peers like China, Brazil, and South Africa by 2–4%.

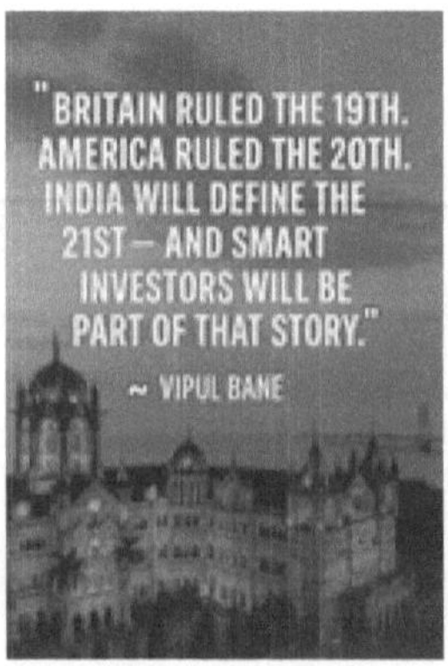

- **Young demographic:** Median age ~28 (one of the youngest in the world), with a workforce of over 900 million.
- **Urbanisation & digital penetration:** Rapid formalisation of economy, Digitalisation, UPI revolution, GST compliance.
- **Stable Macroeconomics**: Low inflation, improving fiscal discipline, forex reserves > $600B.
- **The world's fourth-largest economy** by nominal GDP and third largest by purchasing power parity (PPP).

Why Indian Equities Are Attractive ?

- India's Nifty 50 and Nifty 500 have delivered a CAGR of 12.6% and 13.6% respectively, over the last 10 years. (as of 10th Nov 2025).
- Mid and small caps show even stronger long-term returns — albeit with volatility.
- Strong banking, IT, manufacturing, pharma, and infrastructure sectors are driving growth.
- Increasing SIP inflows — Monthly SIP inflows of a record high 29,529 Crore in October 2025 and a continued increase in retail investor participation show rising trust in equities.
- Stable government, consistent economic policies, and continuing economic reforms such as Jan-Dhan-Aadhaar-Mobile (JAM) trinity, Goods and Services Tax (GST),

Demonetization, and Insolvency and Bankruptcy Code (IBC).

- Global Companies betting BIG on India. Whether it is Apple, Tesla, Samsung, or Google, all are expanding manufacturing in India.
- Despite steep US tariffs, India's resilience shone through—Diwali 2025 witnessed record sales of over ₹6 lakh crore, up 25% year-on-year.
- India is poised to become the world's 3rd largest economy by 2027-28 and a $ 10 trillion powerhouse by 2030-35.

India vs the West — Compelling Contrasts

1. **The US, Japan, and EU have ageing populations** — India has youth (average age 28 years).
2. **Developed markets face slowing consumption** — India is just entering the mass consumption phase.
3. **Low interest rates abroad = capital seeking growth** — India offers that growth.
4. **Rising infrastructure investment** — multiplier effect on job creation and private sector boom.
5. **Technology adoption** — While the West upgrades, India is leapfrogging into digital-first solutions, driving faster innovation and inclusion.

Can NRIs from the US or Canada Invest in Indian Mutual Funds?

Yes — but with some conditions.

Non-Resident Indians (NRIs) from the US and Canada can invest in Indian Mutual Funds, though the process is more regulated compared to NRIs in other countries. This is mainly because of stringent compliance requirements under the Foreign Account Tax Compliance Act (FATCA) for the US and Canadian regulatory guidelines.

Key Points to Know:

1. **Limited Fund Options** — Not all Indian mutual fund houses accept investments from NRIs based in the US or Canada. Only select AMCs (like HDFC, ICICI, SBI, UTI, etc.) allow them, and usually with additional documentation.
2. **Mandatory FATCA Compliance** — US-based NRIs must submit FATCA declarations and disclose tax residency. This ensures transparency of cross-border investments to the IRS.
3. **KYC and Re-KYC Norms** — NRIs must complete a KYC process with Indian fund houses, often requiring in-person verification or attestation from authorised officials abroad.

4. **Modes of Investment**— Investments can be made through NRE or NRO accounts, in INR only. Redemption proceeds are credited back to the same accounts, with tax implications as per Indian law.

5. **Taxation**— Capital gains tax applies in India, with tax deducted at source (TDS). NRIs must also check their reporting and tax obligations in the US/Canada to avoid double taxation, though India has a DTAA (Double Taxation Avoidance Agreement) with both countries.

"Despite the extra compliance, US and Canadian NRIs are increasingly participating in India due to attractive equity markets and currency diversification benefits."

Client Story: Investing Across Borders

Mukesh Ingle, an HR Leader from Pune, was one of our most disciplined investors—clear about his goals and steady in his approach. Three years ago, he received an exciting career opportunity in the US, and his wife, Renu, also secured a transfer with her MNC. The family relocated and, like most NRIs, paused their SIPs briefly while settling down.

Once they adjusted to their new life, Mukesh updated his residential status and restarted his mutual fund investments in India. Not only that, but with renewed clarity, they doubled their SIP amount recently. Today, even while living abroad, Mukesh and

Renu are firmly on the path to financial freedom—proving that distance doesn't have to disrupt disciplined investing when goals remain clear.

"With the right guidance and consistency, NRIs can continue building wealth in India while pursuing opportunities abroad."

3 Things NRIs Must Do Before Restarting SIPs

1. **Update Residential Status**—Inform your mutual fund house and update KYC with NRI status, FATCA declaration (for US/Canada), and new overseas address.
2. **Use Correct Bank Accounts** — Route all investments through NRE/NRO accounts to ensure compliance and easy repatriation of funds.
3. **Check Taxation & Compliance** — Understand TDS on capital gains in India and reporting requirements in your resident country. Consult a tax consultant or a financial coach to avoid double taxation and stay compliant.

GIFT City – Benefits for NRIs/OCIs/PIOs

Investing in Gujarat International Finance Tech-City (GIFT City) provides NRIs with significant benefits such as:

1. **Flexibility:** GIFT City makes investing in India easier in a wide array of options, from Debt instruments and ULIPs to Global stocks, from AIFs to REITs and INVITs.

2. **Significant Tax Advantages:** Such as Zero TDS, Securities Transaction Tax, Commodities Transaction Tax, and stamp duty.
3. **Liquidity:** Term Deposits are highly liquid, offering shorter tenures without any penalties for early withdrawal.
4. **Ability to transact and repatriate funds in foreign** currencies like USD, GBP, and EUR.
5. **No Tax Filings:** Account holders in GIFT City do not have to file income tax returns in India.

Special Benefits for NRIs from the UAE, Singapore, and Malaysia

When it comes to investing in India, NRIs from the **UAE, Singapore, and Malaysia** enjoy a unique advantage — Relief through DTAA — making them some of the most active contributors to India's investment story.

India has signed Double Taxation Avoidance Agreements (DTAA) with all three countries. This ensures NRIs don't pay tax twice on the same income, providing them with clarity and efficiency in managing their wealth.

1. **UAE:** With zero personal income tax, NRIs in the UAE investing in India only pay taxes as per Indian law (with TDS deducted). This simple framework has made them one of the most consistent investor groups in mutual funds and equities.

2. **Singapore:** As a low-tax jurisdiction, Singapore-based NRIs benefit from DTAA, ensuring their Indian earnings are not taxed again back home.
3. **Malaysia:** Indian-origin families in Malaysia also gain from DTAA provisions, reducing their tax burden and encouraging more cross-border investments.

For NRIs in these countries, India offers a blend of emotional connection and financial opportunity. With favourable taxation treaties, simplified compliance, and high growth prospects, investing in India becomes not just a financial choice but a smart wealth-building strategy.

"India is not just an economy — it's an emerging opportunity."

Client Story: Staying Rooted While Growing Wealth

Arshad and Urvi, a Dubai-based NRI couple, have been steadily investing in Indian mutual funds through the SIP and lump sum options with two clear goals in mind — building a strong retirement corpus and upgrading their home in Mumbai.

For them, Indian equities are more than just a tax-efficient wealth-creation tool. They represent a bridge back home, keeping them financially strong and emotionally connected to India.

"For NRIs, investing in India is not just about returns — it's about staying rooted while securing their future."

How to Ride India's Growth Wave?

India today stands as one of the world's fastest-growing economies, powered by a young workforce, rising consumption, and relentless innovation. For NRIs, this is not just a story to admire from afar — it's a chance to participate in the wealth creation that mirrors India's own rise.

The smartest way to capture this opportunity is:

- Through equities, best accessed via Indian mutual funds. Systematic Investment Plans (SIPs) and Step-Up SIPs help you avoid the pitfalls of timing the market while steadily compounding wealth.
- Diversifying across large, mid, and small caps ensures your portfolio grows in line with India's broad opportunity spectrum. For tax efficiency and regulatory ease, GIFT City offers a gateway designed specifically with NRIs in mind.
- The most important step, however, is to stay invested. Equity returns over the long run reflect India's GDP growth and business dynamism — and with global and domestic investors showing unprecedented trust in Indian markets, the outlook is brighter than ever.

"As an NRI, the choice is clear: don't just believe in India's growth story — invest in it, stay the course, and let time do the rest."

Key Learnings:

1. India offers strong demographic and economic tailwinds.
2. Indian Equity returns over the long term reflect GDP growth and business innovation.
3. Indian markets are increasingly trusted by global and domestic investors.
4. NRIs have regulatory-friendly avenues via GIFT City.
5. Don't just believe in India — invest in it.

PILLAR 4

RETIRE & PASS ON

Retirement isn't the end — it's a new beginning. Plan worry-free living, give meaningfully, and leave behind a legacy that matters.

Chapter 19

Retire Worry-Free – Investment Strategies That Work

"Someone's sitting in the shade today because someone planted a tree a long time ago."

— Warren Buffett

"Retirement is not the end of earning — it's the beginning of planned living."

For most, retirement planning is simply about accumulating a big corpus. But wealth without structure is like a ship without a sail. The real magic lies in how you deploy that wealth — ensuring peace of mind, predictable income, and freedom to enjoy life without financial stress.

This chapter is your blueprint for retiring smartly, not just retiring.

Liquidity is King

As you step into retirement, your biggest need isn't growth — it's access. Emergencies don't knock before entering, and inflation doesn't wait.

Why Liquidity Matters:

- Medical expenses, home repairs, family functions, and sudden travel need ready cash.
- Avoid redeeming equity investments during market downturns.
- Keeps you independent — no need to rely on children or loans.

Rule of Thumb: Always keep 12–18 months of expenses in liquid or ultra-short-term funds or bank FDs. This is your peace-of-mind buffer.

Equity — Still Your Ally

Many believe retirement means exiting equity completely. That's a myth.

You're not planning for a 2-year vacation — you're planning for a 25–30-year journey!

Why Equity Still Matters:

- Helps beat inflation (especially medical inflation).
- Ensures your corpus doesn't shrink in real terms.
- Generates growth to support withdrawals over decades.

Rule of Thumb: Maintain 30%–40% in well-diversified equity mutual funds even in retirement. Rebalance annually.

The 3-Bucket Strategy

A popular strategy that we at Adyanta Financials follow. It's very simple to understand, but difficult to implement for a retiree, as it needs discipline and effort to implement.

Divide your retirement corpus into 3 strategic buckets for clarity and peace:

Bucket	Time Horizon	Investment Type	Purpose
1	0–3 years	Liquid Funds, FDs, Arbitrage	Daily expenses & emergencies
2	3–7 years	Hybrid Funds, Short-term Debt, MIPs	Regular income, low volatility
3	7+ years	Equity Mutual Funds, Balanced Advantage	Growth, wealth preservation

Tip: Replenish Bucket 1 from Bucket 2 annually. Rebalance Bucket 3 periodically.

Client Story: Mrs Nair's Journey to Freedom

At 60, Mrs Nair retired from a PSU job with a ₹1.2 Cr corpus. With Adyanta Financials' help, she created a 3-bucket structure. ₹20L went into liquid and short-term debt. ₹40L in hybrid funds, and ₹60L into diversified equity funds.

She now receives a monthly SWP of ₹40,000, travels annually, and recently funded her grandson's education gift from her growth bucket — without touching her emergency fund.

"Retirement isn't about stopping. It's about starting — on your own terms."

4. SWP — The Game-Changer

Systematic Withdrawal Plan (SWP) is the most tax-efficient, stress-free, and sustainable way to generate post-retirement income.

Why SWP Works Wonders:

- Regular monthly cash flow — like a salary.
- More tax-efficient than interest income.
- Let your corpus remain invested and growing.
- Flexibility to increase or reduce withdrawals
- Allows you to adjust for inflation and withdraw a lump sum for emergencies.

Example: A corpus of ₹1 crore in a balanced fund with a 6% annual SWP = ₹50,000/month — while still leaving room for growth.

Bonus: After 1 year, SWP from equity/hybrid funds attracts only capital gains tax, not income tax slabs.

Client Story: Retirement with Freedom and Fulfilment

Mr Haren Sankhe, a retired General Manager from Mahananda Dairy, wanted his retirement years to be financially worry-free and personally fulfilling. With the help of a structured Systematic Withdrawal Plan (SWP), he created a steady stream of income that covers his regular expenses without stress or uncertainty.

What makes his journey special is that while he enjoys this stable income, his portfolio has also grown significantly over time—proving that financial security and growth can go hand in hand.

Freed from money worries, Mr Sankhe now devotes his time to his passion: wildlife photography. From capturing rare bird species to documenting the beauty of nature, his lens reflects the joy of a retirement well-planned.

As he often says, *"A well-designed plan doesn't just fund your retirement—it gives you the freedom to truly live it."*

Retirement Planning is More Than Money

- Plan for health insurance till age 80+.
- Keep an updated Will and nomination records.
- Discuss legacy and gifting goals with family.
- Focus on purpose post-retirement — hobbies, travel, mentoring, volunteering.
- Maintain an emergency fund — Equivalent to 12 to 24 months of expenses.

Key Learnings:

- Retirement planning isn't about playing it defensive. It's about structuring your wealth for joy, freedom, and dignity.
- Ensure liquidity for peace of mind.
- Retain equity for long-term inflation-beating growth.
- Use the 3-bucket strategy to manage the risk and rewards.
- Deploy SWP for sustainable monthly income.

"Effective retirement planning isn't about regular income—it's about securing freedom, dignity, and peace of mind for the years ahead."

Chapter 20

Give While You are Alive — Simple Strategies to Make it Happen

"We make a living by what we get, but we make a life by what we give."

— Winston Churchill

"It's not just about leaving behind wealth. It's about passing on wisdom, values, and responsibility — while you're still around to witness it."

When we think of inheritance, we usually imagine a Will executed after death. But a growing number of individuals, especially in India, are choosing to transfer wealth while they are still alive — to guide, bless, and witness how it's used.

Done right, wealth transmission during your lifetime can be deeply fulfilling, tax-efficient, and legally sound. Done wrong, it can lead to disputes, regret, or even irreversible mistakes.

Why Consider Giving While You Are Alive?

- **Control:** You can supervise how the wealth is used
- **Avoids disputes:** Less chance of legal battles or emotional drama after you're gone
- **Tax efficiency:** India has no gift tax (under certain conditions)

- **Emotional reward:** You get to see the impact of your generosity
- **Better planning:** Easier to distribute assets as per need and capability

How Much Should You Give?

- Do I have enough for my own retirement and health care?
- Am I gifting from surplus or from savings meant for my future needs?
- Am I enabling or spoiling?
- Can I create milestones or conditions?

To Whom Should You Give?

- **Children** — For education, home buying, marriage, or business seed capital
- **Parents** — For retirement care, medical needs, or to fulfil their dreams
- **Spouse** —Joint ownership of property or financial assets
- **Charity** —Via donations, endowments, or philanthropy
- **Others** — Trusted caretakers, relatives, or lifelong friends (if justified)

Tax-Efficient Ways to Transfer Wealth

Method	Benefits	Caution/Notes
Gift Deeds	Tax-free for relatives; applicable for property or cash	Must be registered; taxable if to non-relatives over ₹50,000
Joint Ownership	Smooth transition, easy access to funds	Legal rights may transfer unintentionally
Family Trusts	Structured distribution and control	Needs legal setup and management
Power of Attorney	Nominee can act on your behalf	Must be legally executed; define scope clearly
Gifting Financial Instruments	Can be done for MFs, FDs, stocks	Needs formal procedures and KYC updates
Charity Donations	Offers tax deductions (80G)	Ensure the organisation is registered and compliant

Gift Mutual Fund Units — A New Way to Share Wealth with Purpose

"Money is temporary, but the habit of growing it is a legacy."

SEBI's new rule (effective 1st Nov. 2025) has opened a thoughtful and convenient way to gift or transfer mutual fund units online — even if they're held in non-demat form. No need to sell units or open a demat account. (ETFs, children, and retirement funds remain excluded.)

What's Changed

Until recently, gifting of securities such as bonds or shares and even mutual fund units through a demat account was easy, but offline mutual funds required cumbersome paperwork.

Now, you can gift or transfer mutual fund units digitally through platforms like CAMS, FinTech, or MF Central — a seamless process that completes in just a couple of days.

Both the sender and receiver must hold folios in the same fund house, and the units must be free from any lien, lock-in, or freeze. If the receiver doesn't have a folio, they can open a zero-balance folio instantly.

Who Can Use It

- Resident Indians and NRIs can both send or receive units.
- Minors, however, cannot.

Why It Matters

- **Legacy in Motion** – Gift not just money, but a growing investment that compounds over time.
- **Tax-Smart Giving** – Gifting within close family is generally exempt; the recipient inherits your holding period and cost basis for capital gains.

- **No Redemption Hassles** – Avoid selling and re-investing; the transfer is direct and efficient.
- **Teach Through Gifting** – A perfect way to help young adults or spouses learn the power of SIPs and long-term investing.

Key Pointers

- Units must be clear of lien or lock-in (e.g., ELSS).
- Both parties must be KYC-verified.
- A short cooling-off period (around 10 days) may apply before redemption.
- Stamp duty is minimal, auto-calculated by the portal.

The Adyanta Perspective

At Adyanta Financials, we see this as more than a transaction — it's a way to pass on financial wisdom and values. Gifting mutual fund units can be a meaningful gesture to:

- Celebrate milestones like marriage, graduation, or a new job.
- Kick-start a spouse's or child's investment journey.
- Create a living legacy that grows with time.

"True wealth isn't just accumulated — it's shared, nurtured, and multiplied."

Client Story: Passing on Wealth, Passing on Joy

Mr Yashavant and Mrs Anita Chaudhari, a retired couple from Mumbai, always believed in living a simple, modest life. Over the years, with careful planning and disciplined investing, they built a corpus strong enough to sustain them comfortably for a lifetime.

With their own financial security assured, the Chaudharis chose to share their wealth meaningfully. Through proper legal structures, they began transferring a part of their assets to their daughters, Aparna and Anamika. This timely support helped their daughters achieve critical milestones in life—without stress or delay.

For the Chaudharis, the real joy lies not just in creating wealth but in watching it empower the next generation.

Their story is one of foresight, responsibility, and fulfillment—proof that wealth, when planned well, becomes a legacy of happiness.

"True wealth isn't just preserved—it's passed on with purpose and love."

Mistakes to Avoid

- Gifting emotionally without financial planning
- Not documenting transfers legally
- Ignoring impact on your own liquidity and taxes
- Giving large amounts without educating the recipient

- Adding names to assets without understanding legal implications
- Not updating nominations and legal documents

Client Story: The Cost of Unplanned Giving

Mr Sinha, out of goodwill, gifted his second property to his elder son. Years later, during a medical emergency, he needed funds and requested his son to sell the property to help. To his dismay, the son refused—the property was legally his.

With no proper documentation or clauses in place, Mr Sinha not only lost access to his wealth but also his peace of mind.

"Giving from the heart is fine—but give with a plan, not just goodwill."

Checklist Before You Give

- Is my own retirement corpus secure?
- Is this recipient financially responsible?
- Have I documented the transfer legally?
- Have I updated all nominations and the Power of Attorney?
- Is the gift aligned with my family values and goals?

Key Learnings:

- Giving is rewarding—but only when it's the right amount, to the right people, at the right time, for the right reason, and in the right way.
- Passing on wealth while you're alive is a beautiful way to empower, educate, and experience your legacy in action.
- It's not just about "who gets what," but about how they use it, and how you prepare them to handle it.
- Plan it. Document it. And above all, align it with your values. Because wealth without wisdom is a burden. But wealth with guidance is a blessing.
- Legacy is Not Just What You Leave. It's What You Build.

Chapter 21

Wills, Legacy & Conversations That Matter

"The greatest legacy we can leave our children is happy memories."

— Og Mandino

"You worked hard for your wealth. Don't let it become a legal battlefield after you're gone."

Planning for the future isn't just about building wealth—it's about ensuring that what you've worked for continues to make a positive impact long after you're gone. Wills, legacy planning, and meaningful conversations with loved ones are the tools that turn intentions into clarity and security.

This chapter explores how thoughtful planning and open dialogue can protect your family, preserve your values, and give you the peace of mind that comes from knowing your legacy is in capable hands.

"Legacy is not about how much you leave, but how clearly you leave it."

Why Every Family Needs a Will

Most people think Wills are only for the ultra-rich. Not true.

If you have dependents, property, or even a bank account, you need a Will. Verbal assurances don't hold up in court.

Will, Nomination, Trust — What's the Difference?

Nomination gives access, not legal ownership.

Will gives legal transfer and clarity on distribution.

Trusts are useful for special children, complex family structures, or large estates.

Registering a Will — Yes or No?

Registration is not mandatory but highly recommended. It adds legal strength and prevents future disputes.

You can register a Will at your local sub-registrar's office. Cost is nominal — impact is massive.

Client Story: A Will That Brought Peace of Mind

Mr Joshi, a retired teacher, often worried about how his savings and property would be divided after his lifetime. He had two children, and though relations were cordial, he didn't want them to face disputes later.

We helped him write a simple will with the help of an Attorney, clearly stating how his assets should be distributed.

A few years later, when he passed away, the family found comfort in the clarity his will provided. There were no legal hassles, no arguments—just a smooth transfer of assets exactly as he had wished. His children often say that their father's foresight not only secured their inheritance but also preserved their bond as a family.

"Writing a will isn't about death—it's about protecting loved ones and giving them peace when they need it most."

Gift & Inheritance Tax Rules in India

- Gifts from relatives are tax-free. For non-relatives, above ₹50,000 is taxable.
- Inheritance is not taxed in India, but income generated from inherited assets is taxable.
- Always document gifts with clear declarations to avoid future confusion.

Legacy Mistakes to Avoid

1. Not creating a legal Will
2. Not updating your Will after major life changes (marriage, birth, death).
3. Multiple properties, no clear ownership documentation.
4. No nominee or outdated nominee details.
5. Keeping your family in the dark about key assets — Nearly 2 Lakhs crore lies unclaimed in banks, EPF, and shares.

"Don't leave behind just money. Leave behind peace."

5-Step Legacy Planning Action Plan

1. Create or update your Will — include all movable and immovable assets.
2. Add proper nominees to all financial instruments (bank, MF, PPF, insurance).
3. Discuss your wishes with your spouse and children.
4. Maintain a digital and physical asset inventory.
5. Revisit your legacy plans every 3 years or after major events.

Key Learnings:

1. A Will is not a luxury — it's a necessity.
2. Nominee ≠ legal heir — a Will ensures rightful transfer.
3. Trusts are valuable for special or complex needs.
4. Inheritance is tax-free, but income from it is not.
5. Your real legacy is peace, not paperwork.

PILLAR 5

ADAPT & EVOLVE

The future belongs to those who evolve. Teach kids, empower Gen Z & Alpha, embrace new trends, and grow with the guidance of a coach.

Chapter 22

Financial Literacy for Kids — Empowering the Next Generation

"Don't just give your kids money; teach them how money works. That's real inheritance."

— Robert Kiyosaki

"Don't just leave wealth for your children. Leave them with the wisdom to handle it."

Money lessons aren't taught in schools — they're lived at home.

The earlier children learn good money habits, the stronger their foundation for a secure and balanced life. As Parents, you are the most influential teachers, the first coaches in your child's life, especially when it comes to money.

You don't need complex tools or heavy lectures to instill lifelong financial values, but just the right financial values and habits.

Raising Money-Smart Kids: 11 Lasting Financial Lessons

The seeds of financial behaviour are sown in childhood. Research shows that by age 7, most children have already developed basic money habits. What kids need is consistent guidance, real-life exposure, and small, practical habits that shape their money mindset.

Here are ten **simple yet powerful ways** to empower your kids financially:

1. **Talk About Money Openly (Age-Appropriate)** — Normalise conversations about money. Instead of saying, "we can't afford this," try, "this isn't in our budget right now." This teaches choice and control, not fear.
2. **Introduce the Concept of Earning** — Even toddlers can earn stars or points for good behaviour, which can later convert into rewards. This builds the mindset that money is earned, not magically available.
3. **Let Them Make Mistakes (and learn)** — If they blow their savings on an impulse toy, let them feel the pinch. Small mistakes at 10 prevent costly ones at 30.
4. **Teach Needs vs. Wants** — This simple but powerful distinction is the foundation of financial wisdom. Needs to sustain life; wants to add flavour. Learning to prioritise will shape every financial decision ahead.
5. **Set Goals and Encourage Saving** — Whether it's a toy, a cycle, or souvenirs for a family trip — let kids save towards something specific. This makes money purposeful and builds delayed gratification.
6. **Use Games, Books & Conversations** — Board games like Monopoly, storybooks on money, or involving kids in family budget talks can make financial literacy fun and

natural. The more they hear, play, and practice, the more confident they'll grow with money.

7. **Introduce the concept of Ikigai** — Teach kids the idea of ikigai, a Japanese philosophy of "reason for being". Help them connect money with purpose, passion, and contribution. This way, they don't just chase wealth, but learn to align financial choices with what makes a life meaningful.
8. **Stay Rooted in Culture and Traditions** — Money lessons should go hand-in-hand with values from our rich culture and traditions—saving before spending, giving before receiving, respecting elders' wisdom, and practising gratitude. This balance of modern financial tools with timeless cultural values builds strong, grounded money habits.
9. **The Four Quadrants of Wealth** — Introduce them early to the four quadrants of wealth:
    - Earning (Income)
    - Saving (Protection)
    - Investing (Growth)
    - Giving (Contribution)

    By learning these quadrants, kids see money not just as cash in hand but as a system that sustains life, supports dreams, and creates impact.

10. **Grocery Shopping Lessons** — Take your kids along when you shop at local stores or supermarkets. Involve them in picking items based on needs versus wants, compare prices, and stick to a budget. It's a simple, practical way to help them understand the value of money and mindful spending.
11. **Investment Awareness Programs for kids** — Parents should motivate kids to join Investment Awareness programs like HDFC AMC's "Mission Mars", where kids learn financial wisdom in 2 hours through fun activities and receive certificates and storybooks.

Together, these 11 lessons make financial literacy not just about handling money — but about living wisely, purposefully, and responsibly.

Parent's Note: Children mirror what they see. The best way to teach is to practice these values and habits yourself.

"Empowering your kids financially isn't about making them money-minded. It's about helping them develop confidence, discipline, and balance — skills that will last a lifetime."

Client Story: Teaching Money Early, Creating Lifelong Habits

Mr and Mrs Parkar always wanted their children, Aarav and Minu, to grow up financially confident. Instead of waiting for them to learn about money in adulthood, they started early—opening a minor savings account for each child and introducing a small Junior SIP. They also used games and simple goal-based exercises to teach budgeting, saving, and delayed gratification.

Over time, Aarav learned to prioritise his savings for a new bicycle, while Minu started tracking her small allowance and contributions to a charity she cared about.

The results were visible: the children began making conscious financial choices, asking questions about investments, and understanding the value of money.

The Parkars say it best: "Empowering our kids with financial knowledge today is the gift that grows with them tomorrow."

"Teach them money young, and you give them the freedom to make it work for life."

Tools to Empower Your Kids

- **Open a Minor Savings Account** – Teach them the basics of saving and give them a sense of financial ownership.
- **Invest in a Junior SIP or Child Gift Fund** – Introduce them to disciplined investing and the power of compounding early.
- **Gift Financial Literacy Books or Games** – Make learning about money fun and practical from a young age.

Financial Values to Inculcate from a Young Age

As parents, you're Not Raising Children. You're Raising Future Adults. If you teach kids about geometry and grammar, why not about gratitude, goals, and growth through money?

Value	Actionable Tip
Gratitude	Practice "thank you" when receiving gifts or money.
Patience	Encourage saving for something instead of buying instantly.
Discipline	Regularly update their savings jar or bank account.
Giving	Celebrate birthdays by donating old toys or clothes.
Awareness	Explain how ATMs and UPI work; that money is earned, not magically available.

"The key factor that will determine your financial future is not the economy but your philosophy."

Involve Your Kids — Build a Budget, Build Their Mindset

*"Tell me, and I forget; teach me, and I remember; involve me, and I learn." — **Benjamin Franklin.***

Budgeting isn't just about balancing numbers — it's about building values.

When you involve your children in preparing your home budget, you're not merely teaching them mathematics; you're showing them the story of money — how it flows, how it's earned, and how it can be used purposefully.

Give them small roles — let them list monthly groceries, track expenses on apps, or compare savings goals. When they see the connection between a weekend pizza and the family's monthly budget, they begin to understand choices and priorities. Over time, this becomes their foundation for financial discipline and gratitude.

Children learn best not through lectures but through participation. By making budgeting a family ritual, you are not just raising smart spenders — you're nurturing future wealth creators who value money, respect effort, and make informed decisions.

"Involve them early — and you won't have to teach them later."

Client Story: When Financial Wisdom Starts at Home

Shweta and Shounak Bhagwate have always been disciplined investors, staying steady through life's ups and downs. But their biggest success isn't just in their portfolio — it's in how they've shaped their son, Shreyansh.

At just 13, Shriansh understands the value of saving, the difference between needs and wants, and the importance of earning his way through merit. His financial awareness reflects the lessons learned at home — lessons of responsibility, clarity, and balance.

"Financial literacy isn't taught — it's caught. Kids learn best when parents lead by example."

Your Turn — The Family Budget Circle

This weekend, make your budgeting session a family ritual.

Here's how:

- List together your family's top 5 monthly expenses.
- Ask your kids to suggest where savings can happen — you'll be amazed at their creativity!
- Set a small family goal (e.g., saving for a short trip or a new board game).
- Track it visually — use a chart, jar, or app. Let kids decorate it!

Then, discuss what they learned about needs vs wants, patience vs impulse, and gratitude vs greed.

"How did your child react when involved in budgeting? What surprised you the most about their perspective on money?"

Key Learnings:

- Start **Early:** Introducing money concepts early helps children build a strong foundation and lifelong financial habits.
- Make it **Practical:** Use real-life examples, allowances, and small investments to teach budgeting and saving.
- Teach **Goal-Based Saving:** Help children set short-term and long-term financial goals to instill purpose-driven habits.
- Encourage **Decision-Making:** Allow kids to make simple financial choices to build confidence and responsibility.
- Leverage **Tools:** Minor savings accounts, Junior SIPs, and educational games make learning interactive and fun.
- Lead **by Example:** Children emulate parents—model good financial behaviour consistently.
- Focus **on Values, Not Just Money:** Teach generosity, delayed gratification, and mindful spending alongside saving and investing.

Chapter 23

Start Early, Stay Wise – Strategies for Gen Z

"Small habits, when started young, compound into big freedoms later."

— James Clear

"The best time to start was yesterday. The next best time is now."

Gen Z is digital, diverse, and dynamic — yet increasingly anxious about money.

A recent survey found that **70% of Indian Gen Z feel stressed about finances**, from student loans to lifestyle pressure.

Gen Alpha, the children of millennials, will grow up in an even faster, more digitally connected world.

For both generations, financial awareness does not begin with complex jargon — it begins with a few simple truths:

- **Money is a tool, not a trophy:** Spending to impress will drain you; spending with purpose will empower you.
- **Discipline is the Key:** 60% of Gen Z track spending on apps, but less than 30% invest systematically.
- **Psychology of money:** Learning delayed gratification early reduces impulse spending by up to 40% in later years.

Even starting small can create a big impact. A ₹1,000 monthly SIP started at age 20 could grow to **over ₹20 lakh by 40,** assuming a 12% CAGR—thanks to compounding.

From Finfluencers to Financial Discipline

The internet is awash with advice—Finfluencers, YouTube gurus, crypto hype—but not all of it is wisdom. Blindly following trends leads to **FOMO losses** and stress.

Keep it real:

- Avoid FOMO: Hype fades, losses linger.
- Understand before you act: No shortcuts—clarity first.
- Stay invested, not addicted: Speculation is not a shortcut to wealth.
- Start Goal-Based SIPs: For your top 3 financial goals
- Seek Professional Help: To stay focused and disciplined

"Simplicity scales. Consistency compounds."

Client Story: Ananya's Head Start

Ananya, 23, an electronics engineer and daughter of my friend and client Aditi Pikale from the UK, became financially independent while still completing her degree.

Inspired by her parents' discipline, she started investing from her very first salary — choosing systematic, goal-based SIPs over impulse spending.

With ambition and clarity, she is building her financial roadmap early, determined to live on her terms and retire young.

"The earlier you start, the easier financial freedom becomes."

The Starter Toolkit

Every young adult should build a basic financial toolkit:

- **Emergency Fund** – 3–6 months of living expenses in a liquid fund or FD.
- **Mutual Fund SIPs** – Start with as little as ₹1000. Increase contributions with income growth.
- **Term Insurance (if earning)** – Affordable coverage that protects against uncertainties.
- **Health Insurance** – Even if young and healthy, medical emergencies are unpredictable.
- **Budgeting Tools** – Apps like Walnut, Jupiter, or simple Google Sheets.
- **Safe Investments** – Digital gold, index funds, or short-term debt funds for beginners.

"Automate savings. Make it a habit, not a headache."

Client Story: Starting Early, Living Freely

Arya More, after completing her graduation and master's in the UK, returned to India and began her career in an export firm. Unlike her mother, who only began structured investments in her 40s, Arya took a different path.

At just 26, she created a clear financial roadmap and started goal-based SIPs. Her vision is simple yet powerful — achieve financial independence early and design a life of choice, not compulsion.

Her story reflects the new mindset of Gen Z: start early, invest smartly, and buy freedom with time.

"Clarity plus early action turns dreams into achievable goals."

Side Hustle to Wealth Engine

Many Gen Zers in India earn via content creation, freelance gigs, or even part-time jobs. But money earned ≠ , money kept.

The 50-30-20 Rule for Side Hustles:

- 50% Spend
- 30% Invest
- 20% Upskill

Reinvest in tools, courses, or mentors. Lifestyle inflation is the silent wealth killer. Your side hustle should fund freedom, not just fun.

The Marshmallow Test: Why Gen Z Must Master the Art of Waiting

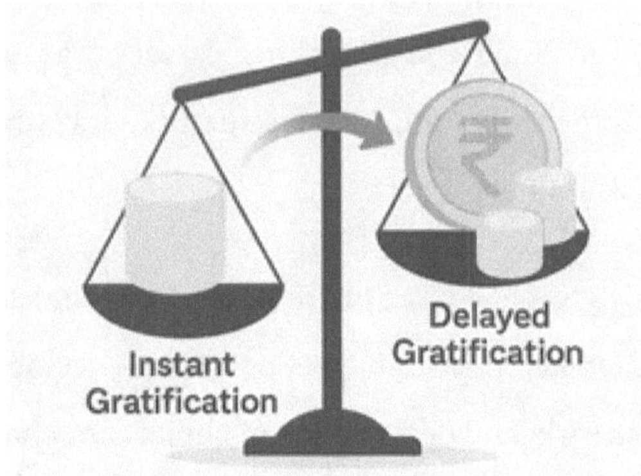

In the late 1960s, psychologist Walter Mischel conducted the now-famous Marshmallow Experiment at Stanford University. Children were offered one marshmallow immediately, or two if they could wait for 15 minutes.

Years later, researchers found that those who waited scored higher on academic tests, had better emotional control, and achieved greater success in life.

The lesson was timeless — delayed gratification often leads to lasting rewards.

Fast forward to today's Gen Z — a generation born into instant likes, one-click deliveries, and dopamine-driven apps. In a world of quick thrills, the ability to delay gratification is a superpower — especially in personal finance.

Take, for instance, **Anish Patil,** a 22-year-old software engineer

from Mumbai. While many of his peers spend their first salary on gadgets or weekend trips, Anish channels 30% into SIPs.

His friends enjoy instant pleasures, but Anish enjoys compounding — the quiet magic that multiplies wealth invisibly, year after year. Twenty-five years later, that "boring" decision could mean financial freedom before 50.

Whether it's resisting impulsive online shopping, choosing SIP over EMIs, or saying no to the latest iPhone and saying yes to early retirement, the modern marshmallow isn't candy anymore; it's money.

Your Turn: The Power of Patience

Take a pause and reflect:

- Where in your financial life are you seeking instant gratification?
- What "second marshmallow" could you earn by waiting, saving, or investing wisely today?
- Could your next financial decision compound into freedom tomorrow?

"The real reward isn't in the wait — it's in who you become while waiting."

Key Learnings

- **Financial purpose beats financial products.** Know why you're investing.
- **Start early.** Starting 10 years earlier can double your retirement corpus
- **Discipline is everything.** Consistent, goal-based investing creates wealth and freedom.
- **Create a Financial Roadmap:** A Vision for the future, along with your values, is crucial for success.
- **Validate before you follow.** Technology is for learning and convenience, not for taking unverified advice.

"Start small, stay consistent, and let time do the heavy lifting."

Chapter 24

Investment Trends and the Future of Wealth Creation

"The best way to predict the future is to create it."

— Peter Drucker

"Markets will evolve. So should your strategy. But your purpose must remain timeless."

The Indian investment journey has transformed radically. We've moved from the era of Fixed Deposits (FDs), gold savings, and LIC policies to a time dominated by SIPs in Mutual Funds, ETFs, MLDs, REITs, and now Specialised Investment Funds (SIFs).

Technology, accessibility, and rising financial literacy have brought more retail investors into the market. Today's young investors begin their journey with apps, UPI, and digital onboarding — a far cry from the physical forms and long queues of the past.

Key Emerging Trends

- **Passive Investing Boom**: Index funds and ETFs are gaining popularity due to lower costs and reliable performance.
- **GIFT City Revolution:** NRIs and resident Indians can now access global markets more efficiently.
- **ESG Investing:** Environmental, Social, and Governance (ESG) funds allow investing with a conscience.
- **Thematic & AI-driven Funds:** Focused funds on megatrends like EVs, AI, green energy, and tech.
- **Fractional Real Estate & REITs:** Owning real estate exposure without the capital burden of full ownership.

- **Crypto & Blockchain:** Although highly volatile and speculative, blockchain technology could reshape finance.
- **International Funds:** Investors are increasingly looking at international funds to diversify across global economies amid rising geopolitical tensions
- **Commodities:** Gold and silver ETFs have seen renewed interest following last year's boom.
- **Robo-advisory platforms** powered by AI and chatbots are making investing faster, smarter, and more accessible than ever.

The Rise of Personalisation

Financial planning is no longer one-size-fits-all. With advancements in technology, risk profiling, and behavioural analytics, portfolios can now be customised to individual goals, risk tolerance, and even spending behaviour.

Robo-advisory platforms offer algorithm-driven suggestions, while human financial coaches continue to provide empathy and experience-based insights.

The best approach? A hybrid one.

Suggestions from Robo-Advisory and personalisation, guidance and execution through a trusted advisor or coach.

Client Story: From DIY to Future-Ready Wealth

For years, Manish Lokhande was a disciplined saver and a do-it-yourself investor. He managed his finances well, but in 2022, when we created a comprehensive Financial Roadmap and walked him and his wife, Smita, through it, they discovered something eye-opening—hidden blind spots and untapped opportunities that had gone unnoticed.

Armed with this clarity, the couple shifted gears. Over the last three years, they've built a strong, diversified, and goal-based portfolio—one that not only reflects today's market realities but is also positioned smartly for the future. Their investments now span multiple asset classes, combining safety with growth, and stability with innovation.

With a roadmap to guide them and a portfolio aligned to both present trends and future opportunities, Manish and Smita are now on the fast track to achieving their dreams and Financial Freedom—earlier than they ever imagined.

"A clear roadmap and a guide turn good savers into free achievers."

Future Is Multi-Asset, Global & Agile

Diversification is no longer just equity vs. debt. Today's and tomorrow's smart portfolios will include:

- Domestic and international equity
- Fixed income, gold, and real estate (including REITs and InvITs)
- Alternate assets like SIFs, global ETFs, and digital assets
- Data-driven investing, tactical allocation, and periodic reviews will become standard practice.

India's long-term growth potential — fueled by demographics, digitalisation, and entrepreneurship — makes it a compelling investment destination for decades to come.

Client Story: Staying Ahead with Future-Ready Investments

When Vishaldeep Gupta began his Financial Freedom journey with us in 2022, one thing was clear—he wasn't just another investor; he was a student of the markets. Disciplined, knowledgeable, and always curious about emerging trends, he often engages in deep conversations with us about how the future of investing is evolving.

With this mindset, his portfolio today reflects the best of traditional and new-age opportunities. Spread across Mutual Funds, PMS, Pre-IPO investments, IAP, and P2P Lending, it is a living example of how diversification—when guided by foresight—can unlock superior growth.

The results speak for themselves. Vishaldeep's portfolio has consistently outperformed broader markets, giving him not just financial returns but also confidence that he is ahead of the curve. With the blend of discipline and future-ready strategies, we are certain he is on track to achieve Financial Freedom earlier than he ever imagined.

Lesson: Wealth creation in the future won't be about chasing trends blindly—it will be about combining discipline with smart diversification into emerging opportunities.

"Tomorrow's wealth is created today—by those who invest ahead of the curve."

How Should Investors Prepare?

1. **Stay informed** but don't get swayed by noise.
2. **Use tech tools** but validate their advice.
3. **Focus on long-term goals,** not short-term fads.
4. **Keep your portfolio diversified** and reviewed.
5. Most importantly, **build financial discipline** and patience.

"Remember, the tools will change. Trends will come and go. But the principles of investing — clarity, discipline, and goal orientation — will never go out of style."

Chapter 25

Why a Financial Advisor or Coach and a Clear Roadmap Are Essential Today?

"A coach is someone who tells you what you don't want to hear, so you can be who you want to be."

— Tom Landry

"A goal without a plan is just a wish." — ***Antoine de Saint-Exupéry***

What is a Financial Plan?

A financial plan is a strategic roadmap that aligns your money with your life goals. It covers all aspects of your financial journey — from budgeting, saving, investing, insurance, tax planning, to retirement and estate planning.

Think of it as your Google Maps for wealth creation — showing where you are, where you want to go, and how to get there most efficiently.

A well-crafted financial plan includes:

- Clear goal-setting (education, home, retirement, etc.)
- Current financial health assessment (income, expenses, assets, liabilities)
- Investment strategy (asset allocation, SIPs, lump sum deployment)
- Risk management (insurance, emergency fund)
- Tax optimisation
- Milestone tracking and course correction

Need for a Financial Plan

In a world full of financial noise — crypto trends, F&O tips, insurance agents posing as planners — most individuals are lost without a compass. A financial plan gives clarity, confidence, and control.

Without it, you're:

- Chasing random returns instead of purpose-driven goals
- Reacting emotionally to market noise
- Overexposed to risks you don't even understand
- Missing tax-saving opportunities
- Living paycheck to paycheck despite a decent income

Why Create It with a Professional?

S.no	Goals	Cost of Goals	Future Value	Existing Assets	Monthly SIP
1	Child Graduation (2035)	3000000	6476775	6497041	
2	Child Post Graduation (2038)	4000000	10878495	10904254	
3	Retirement (2038)		14939645	30045371	25685
4	Home Renovation (2028)	200000	245009	245862	
5	Purchase of Shop (2028)	700000	857530	859816	

6	Second home (2032)	1000000	1605781	1209243	2371
7	Car Upgrade (2029)	1500000	1966194		28151
8	Business Capital (2031)	500000	750365		5812

Real-life example of GAP Analysis and Monthly Cost of Goals of one of our clients (Assuming inflation at 7% and Mutual Fund return at 12% CAGR)

You may be smart. But a smart investor knows when to hire a guide. Here's why partnering with a financial coach or advisor makes a massive difference:

1. **Objectivity:** Professionals aren't emotionally attached to your money. They bring logic, not impulse.
2. **Expertise:** From tax laws to asset allocation to inflation-adjusted planning — they stay updated, so you don't have to.
3. **Customisation:** No one-size-fits-all. A planner helps you align your plan with your goals, risk appetite, and life stage.
4. **Behavioural Coaching:** The biggest threat to wealth isn't poor returns — it's poor decisions. A good advisor helps you stay disciplined.
5. **Accountability:** Just like a fitness coach, a financial planner keeps you on track and ensures you follow through.

Benefits of a Structured Financial Plan

- **Peace of Mind** — No more sleepless nights over money
- **Goal Clarity** — You know exactly how much to save, for what, and by when
- **Optimised Returns** — Not the highest returns, but the right returns for the right goals
- **Risk Mitigation** — Adequate protection with insurance and diversification
- **Wealth Creation** — Systematic and sustainable growth over the years
- **Legacy Planning** — Ensure your wealth passes on efficiently

Client Story: From Financial Anxiety to Freedom

Aditi and Sunil Pawar, a working couple from Thane, had what many would call a "complete" financial life—savings, investments, and insurance. Yet, beneath the surface, anxiety lingered. Were they saving enough for their child's education? Would retirement be comfortable? Could they afford their dream home?

When they approached us, we crafted a comprehensive financial plan that aligned every rupee with their life goals. Within six months, their scattered finances were transformed into a clear, actionable roadmap.

Five years on, the results speak volumes: they live in their dream home, their investments are on track, and financial stress is a thing of the past. Most importantly, Aditi pursued her passion—leaving her corporate job to become an Assistant Professor, while also working toward her PhD.

"A clear plan doesn't just secure your finances—it frees your life."

AI Apps vs Financial Advisors or Coaches

"Tools Can Assist. Only Humans Can Guide."

The AI revolution has transformed investing.

Today, a corporate professional can start a SIP during a coffee break

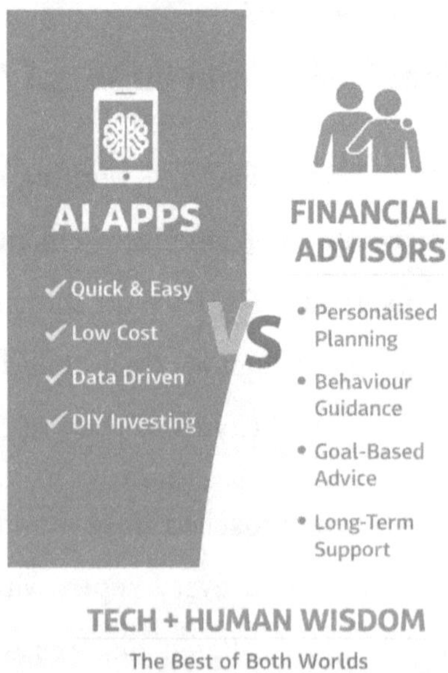

An NRI can track Indian investments from across continents.

A Gen Z investor can compare hundreds of funds with a swipe.

AI-enabled investment apps have made **access frictionless**—and that is a major achievement.

But access alone does not guarantee outcomes.

What AI Apps Do Exceptionally Well

Investment apps excel at execution and efficiency.

They offer:

- Speed and convenience
- Low-cost or zero-commission investing
- Data-rich dashboards and analytics
- Automated SIPs and reminders
- Easy fund discovery and comparisons

For disciplined investors with simple goals, these tools are valuable.

They answer the question: "How do I invest?"

Where Technology Reaches Its Limits

Despite powerful tools, many investors still:

- Panic during market corrections
- Chase last year's top-performing funds
- Over-allocate to fashionable themes
- Ignore asset allocation and review discipline
- Make tax-inefficient or poorly timed decisions

These are not data problems.

They are decision-making problems.

AI can process numbers.

It cannot fully process context, emotions, or life complexity.

The Distinct Role of a Financial Advisor or Coach

A financial advisor does not replace technology.

They provide what technology cannot.

1. Contextual Judgment

Advisors interpret data through the lens of your career stage, family responsibilities, cross-border realities (for NRIs), and life priorities.

2. Behavioural Guardrails

They help investors stay invested when fear dominates—and stay grounded when greed takes over.

3. Integration Over Isolation

Apps view investments in silos. Advisors integrate investments with insurance, taxation, cash flows, and long-term goals.

4. Personalisation Beyond Profiles

Two people with identical incomes and ages can—and should—have different strategies. Advisors design for the person, not the algorithm.

5. Continuity and Accountability

Markets change. Life changes faster. Advisors provide ongoing recalibration—not one-time recommendations.

A False Debate

The real question is not: **AI Apps or Financial Advisors/Coaches?**

The better question is: **How do you combine efficiency with wisdom?**

AI is a powerful tool.

A financial advisor or Coach is a guide.

The most resilient investors use technology for execution and rely on advisors for direction.

Why Advisors/Coaches Remain Relevant in the AI Age

As information becomes abundant, clarity becomes scarce.

The future of wealth creation will not be decided by who has the most data—but by who makes the **fewest behavioural mistakes**

over long periods of time.

And that is where human guidance continues to matter.

Use apps.

But don't outsource judgment.

"Technology can help you invest faster.

Wisdom helps you invest better—and stay invested longer."

Financial Advisor vs Financial Coach: Key Differences

Although the terms financial advisor and financial coach are often used interchangeably, they serve very different roles in an investor's journey.

A financial advisor typically focuses on products, strategies, and execution — helping you choose investments, insurance, or retirement plans tailored to your goals.

A financial coach, on the other hand, works on the foundation: your money mindset, behaviours, and habits. The coach helps you build discipline, clarity, and confidence so that the advice you eventually act upon creates lasting results.

In short, an advisor tells you where to invest, while a coach ensures you are ready to invest wisely.

The 5 Key differences can be summarised as below:

Parameter	Financial Advisor	Financial Coach
Role Focus	Provides advice on investments, insurance, retirement plans, etc.	Holistic. Helps build financial habits, mindset, and goal clarity.
Approach	Product/portfolio-oriented	Behavioural/goal-oriented
Client Relationship	Transactional; focuses on managing money	Transformational; focuses on client empowerment
Education & Awareness	Limited; assumes client follows advice	High aims to educate and build long-term financial behaviour
Goal	Optimise returns and manage risk	Achieve financial independence or Freedom through habits and clarity

In practice, financial advisors often play the role of a coach—and coaches frequently offer advisory guidance.

What matters is whether they bring clarity, discipline, and alignment between your money and your life.

"Choose guidance that builds Confidence- not just portfolios"

Does Everyone Need a Financial Coach?

Not really.

If you're confident about your financial decisions, on track with your goals, and genuinely content with where you are, then you probably don't need one.

But if you're curious to learn more, want to avoid costly mistakes, seek an unbiased perspective, or are looking to retire early, live stress-free, or simply make your money work harder and smarter, then a financial coach could be your biggest asset.

Think of it like fitness. You don't need a personal trainer to stay fit. But if you want to break through plateaus, follow a proven routine, or stay consistently accountable—a coach helps you get there faster, better, and with fewer detours.

A financial coach isn't for everyone.

But for the right people, they can change everything. A financial coach narrows the 2.5% -5% gap by replacing emotion with discipline and strategy in every investment decision. In addition to the right strategy, products and reviews, the coach can further add 2.5% to 5% value to your financial future besides saving your valuable time and efforts.

"A Financial Coach does help you avoid costly money mistakes and add significant value to your investment portfolio, but Peace of mind is the ultimate alpha."

Client Story: The Power of a Roadmap and a Coach

Since 2018, Amit Barve and his wife, Dr Rashmi, have been following the Financial Roadmap we designed for them with discipline and clarity. With every step, periodic reviews, and consistent coaching, they've turned aspirations into achievements.

One of the biggest milestones has been Dr Rashmi fulfilling her dream of setting up her own Eye Clinic in a prime location in Thane—a goal once distant, now a proud reality. Their journey proves how a well-directed plan, combined with the guidance of a coach, can fast-track success.

Today, Amit and Rashmi are not only achieving goals one after another but are also firmly on course toward their ultimate destination—Financial Freedom.

"A Financial coach doesn't just guide your money—they accelerate your dreams."

How to Choose the Right Financial Coach

Because choosing the right guide matters more than choosing the right fund.

In a world full of financial influencers and product sellers, a true financial coach stands apart — not by promising high returns, but by offering clarity, discipline, and direction. Choosing the right coach can make the difference between chasing returns and achieving real financial freedom.

When selecting your financial coach, look beyond numbers. Look for someone who listens before advising, who simplifies instead of complicating, and who stays available not just in good times but especially during crises.

A good coach offers role clarity, transparency, and measurable progress, helping you align every decision with your life goals — not with market noise.

Here's a simple checklist:

- **Services & Role Clarity** — Do they act as your guide or just a product distributor?
- **Availability in Crisis** — Are they reachable when you need them most?
- **Fee Transparency** — Do you clearly know how they earn?
- **Performance Benchmarks** — Do they track your goals, not just returns?
- **Referrals** — What do their existing clients say?

Avoid coaches who overpromise returns, push products, or focus on how they make money — not how you grow it.

"A good financial coach doesn't sell you dreams — they help you live them."

The 7-Step Path to Financial Freedom

1. **Clarity of Goals**

   → Know what you want. Be Specific. A vague goal leads to vague results.

2. **Household Budgeting — Setting Financial Ratios and Debt Optimisation**

   → Track, optimise, and align your spending with what truly matters. Use debt wisely.

3. **Asset Allocation**

   → The Right Asset Mix. Based on your goals, risk profile and current financial situation.

4. **Strategic Investments Aligned to Goals**

   → No random bets. Invest with purpose and a personalised asset allocation plan.

5. **Protect your Goals — Emergency Fund & Insurances**

   → Safeguard your journey from unforeseen shocks. Shield before you wield.

6. **Build Passive Income and Wealth Transmission Plan**

   → Let your money multiply. And plan how it lives beyond you.

7. Periodic Reviews & Rebalancing

→ Life changes. So should your plan. Track, tweak, and stay on course.

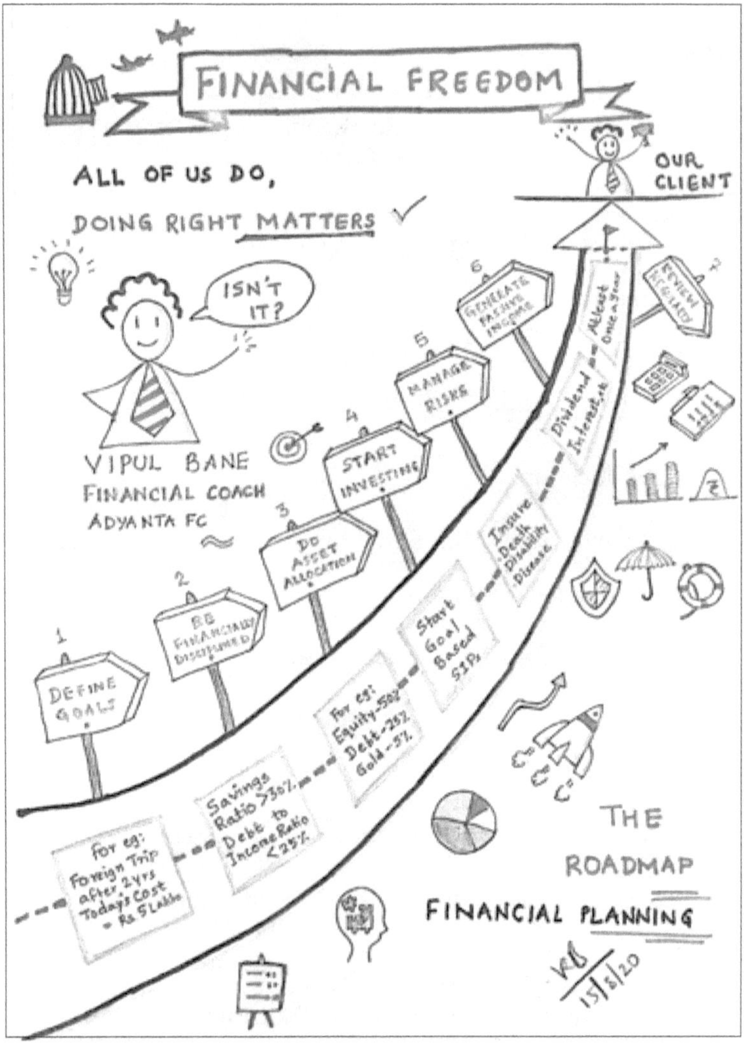

This isn't theory—it's a framework that has helped 1000+ individuals and families take control of their money, reduce financial stress, and live richer, more meaningful lives.

And you could be next.

The Cost of Hiring a Financial Coach

Many people hesitate to hire a Financial Coach, assuming it's an unnecessary expense. But in reality, the cost of not having one is often far greater. A Financial Coach doesn't just manage investments — they bring structure, discipline, and clarity to your entire financial life.

They help you avoid costly mistakes such as misaligned insurance, poor tax planning, random investing, or chasing market fads — errors that can silently erode lakhs of rupees over time.

When you hire a Financial Coach, you're not paying for products or quick tips — you're investing in strategy, accountability, and peace of mind.

Just as you wouldn't hesitate to pay a doctor or a fitness coach for your health, a financial coach ensures your wealth remains healthy and purposeful. The small fee you pay today often saves you multiples of it tomorrow — in taxes, wrong decisions, and lost opportunities. In that sense, a good coach doesn't cost; they pay for themselves many times over.

At Adyanta Financials, we believe coaching works best when values align. That's why **we don't charge any upfront fees** — instead, we choose to work with clients who reflect our five core principles: shared values, commitment, mutual respect, transparency, and an openness to learn.

The only additional cost, if you're currently investing in direct funds, would be less than 1% (the net difference in expense ratios) —but the tangible value we can add to your financial life can easily exceed 5%.

"A Financial Coach is not an expense — it's an insurance against financial confusion and investment in clarity, confidence, and lifelong freedom."

Key Learnings:

- A financial plan isn't a luxury. It's a necessity.
- And just like you wouldn't perform surgery on yourself or fight a legal case without a lawyer, don't leave your financial future to DIY guesses.
- An advisor or Coach who has been there, done that, can help you achieve your goals faster and easier.
- If you are disciplined and focused, an advisor can help, but if you want to build the right financial habits and achieve financial freedom, seek the help of a Financial Coach.
- In any case, partner with a professional, craft your roadmap and walk confidently toward financial freedom

PILLAR 6

REFLECT & APPLY

True freedom comes from applied knowledge. Avoid pitfalls, act on lessons, follow mantras and action plans, and discover freedom beyond money.

Chapter 26

Beware the Pitfalls — Danger Zones and Common Mistakes in Investing

"It's not what you earn, it's what you keep that makes you rich."

— Robert Kiyosaki

"Success in money often comes not from doing everything right, but from avoiding what goes wrong."

In personal finance and investing, bright professionals often earn well and invest regularly, yet fall short of their goals—not from lack of effort, but from repeating a few critical mistakes.

Think of it like driving — you don't need to know every road, but you must know the accident-prone zones.

Similarly, in money matters, there are **"danger zones"** in investing and common mistakes in day-to-day money management. Knowing them can save you years of regret:

Who Should Do Trading — and Who Shouldn't?

Trading = High-risk, high-stress.

Suitable for:

- Seasoned professionals with deep market knowledge
- Those with time, temperament, tools, and technical know-how
- People using only surplus funds they can afford to lose

Not suitable for:

- Salaried individuals with financial responsibilities
- Emotionally driven or impatient investors

- Those without risk management systems

"If you're not doing it full-time with full knowledge, don't do it at all."

Why F&O Trading Can Destroy Your Wealth

- Futures & Options (F&O) are leveraged instruments — small mistakes = big losses
- Often used by retail investors without proper hedging or strategy
- Most retail F&O traders lose money due to:
  - Greed and overconfidence
  - Lack of risk control
  - Chasing quick profits

Statistics Check: NSE data shows 9 out of 10 retail F&O traders end up in losses.

"Don't risk decades of savings to earn a few quick bucks."

Client Story: The Turning Point

Sunil's foray into Futures & Options ended in heavy losses and sleepless nights. At his boss's suggestion, he reached out to us.

We created a financial roadmap tailored to his family's needs, giving him clarity and direction. Starting with small SIPs, he gradually aligned his money with his goals instead of speculation.

Today, Sunil owns his dream home and enjoys peace of mind—proof that a solid financial plan and the right coach can turn setbacks into success.

"A clear plan and the right coach turn losses into lasting success."

Why Crypto Shouldn't Be in Your Core Portfolio

- Highly volatile and largely unregulated
- Price moves are often based on speculation, not fundamentals
- Regulatory uncertainty in India and globally

Smart Approach:

- Allocate <5% of surplus capital, not core funds
- Treat it as an experiment, not a stable investment

"Don't put what you can't afford to lose into crypto."

How to Identify Ponzi Schemes & Stay Away

Protect Yourself:

- Check for SEBI/RBI registration
- Avoid schemes promising fixed returns from risky markets

- Ask: "Where is the real revenue being generated?"
- Avoid cash or third-party payments
- Beware of Investment red flags

"If it sounds too good to be true, it probably is."

Client Story: The Trap of Easy Money

Mr Shrinivasan, a retired professional from an Indian MNC, had secured his retirement with a steady SWP. One day, a glossy ad on social media caught his attention — a trading group promising unusually high returns.

Curious, he clicked the link and joined a WhatsApp group. At first, the trades looked profitable, and he kept adding more money.

But when he tried to withdraw, the app collapsed and the group disappeared. At the cybercrime cell, he learned it was a fake platform — many had lost lakhs, some crores.

The financial loss hurt, but the guilt and shame of the online fraud cut deeper. His story is a stark reminder: in investing, easy money often comes at the highest cost.

"Chasing quick gains can cost your hard-earned wealth—stay disciplined and alert."

How to Avoid Online Financial Frauds

Precautions:

- Never share OTPs, passwords, or PINs
- Enable 2FA (Two-Factor Authentication)
- Be alert to phishing emails or urgent links
- Avoid unknown apps and unsolicited calls
- Use secure connections and devices

Must-Dos:

- Use official banking and investment apps
- Regularly check SMS/email alerts
- Immediately freeze accounts if suspicious activity occurs

"If someone is rushing you to act — pause and verify."

Avoid Comparison and Fear of Missing Out (FOMO)

Don't compare your financial journey, status, or portfolio with others — their situation, risk profile, and goals are different from yours.

How to Stay on Track:

- Set clear money goals
- Understand your risk profile
- Maintain realistic expectations

Even FOMO can be managed with a solid financial plan — your north star for investing decisions, regardless of market hype.

"Regular reviews with a professional help track progress and clarify portfolio performance."

Avoid Multiple Financial Advisors

Having too many advisors can create confusion, conflicting advice, and unnecessary complexity in your financial planning.

Why it's risky:

- Different advisors may recommend contradictory strategies
- Hard to track your overall portfolio and goals
- Can lead to over-diversification or duplicated investments

Smart Approach:

- Choose **one trusted, qualified advisor** who understands your goals and risk profile
- Maintain **regular reviews** and ask for clear, actionable guidance

- Take responsibility for understanding your own investments

"Multiple voices can cloud your judgment — clarity comes from focus."

Client Story: Too Many Cooks, Spoil the Broth

Subhash, a Senior VP in an MNC, had a large investment portfolio—but no direction. With three different advisors from Anand Rathi, Motilal Oswal, and IIFL, each managing their slice independently, the result was chaos: overlapping funds, asset mismatch, and conflicting advice.

When he approached us for an unbiased review, we consolidated and realigned everything with his goals.

Five years later, his streamlined portfolio delivers a consistent 5% alpha—and Subhash is on track to retire five years early.

"When advice multiplies, clarity divides. Choose one coach, not many consultants."

Overlooking Tax Planning

Ignoring taxes can silently erode your investment returns over time. Many investors focus only on returns without factoring in **capital gains, income tax, or deductions.**

Smart Approach:

- Factor in taxes while planning investments
- Use tax-efficient instruments such as ELSS, PPF, NPS, or SIP-based mutual funds
- Plan withdrawals and redemptions considering tax implications

"Tax planning is not optional — it's a silent wealth multiplier."

Chasing Market Hype

Buying "hot stocks" or following media-fuelled trends often leads to emotional investing, resulting in buying high and selling low.

Smart Approach:

- Stick to a **long-term investment strategy**
- Diversify across asset classes and follow your risk profile
- Avoid impulsive decisions based on short-term news

"Short-term excitement can destroy long-term wealth. Patience beats hype."

DIY Without Expertise — When Confidence Outruns Competence

Online platforms have made investing look simple, but easy access doesn't equal expertise. Many DIY investors mistake information for understanding — chasing returns, timing markets, or reacting to trends without a clear roadmap.

Without guidance on risk, asset allocation, and discipline, what begins as independence often ends in frustration. A financial coach helps balance emotion with logic and keeps you focused when markets waver.

"DIY without expertise isn't empowerment — it's exposure."

Client Story — From DIY to a purposeful portfolio

Mr Shivanand Ruikar, a senior citizen from Mumbai, loved trading and had built a portfolio of over 100 stocks — but without any real analysis or direction. When we reviewed it, returns were far below potential.

We streamlined his holdings to 20 quality stocks and shifted the rest to Mutual Funds and PMS. Within three years, his portfolio delivered over 15% CAGR — with zero NPAs and complete peace of mind.

After his passing in March 2025, the wealth transition to his wife and son was seamless, a testament to the power of disciplined planning.

"In investing, focus and structure create freedom — not frenzy."

Lack of Contingency Planning

Life is unpredictable. Emergencies, health crises, or job loss can derail even the best-laid financial plans. Many investors fail because they over-rely on future income.

Smart Approach:

- Maintain an emergency fund covering 6–12 months of expenses
- Have adequate insurance coverage (health, life, critical illness)
- Include contingency thinking in your financial plan

"An emergency fund and insurance aren't optional — they're your financial safety net."

Self-Reflection Quiz: Are You Falling into Investing Danger Zones?

Answer **Yes or No** to the following:

1. Do you often act on stock tips from friends, social media, or the news without research?
2. Do you have more than one financial advisor giving you conflicting advice?
3. Have you ever invested in something just because it was "hot" or trending?

4. Do you ignore tax implications when making investment decisions?
5. Do you currently have an emergency fund that covers at least 6 months of expenses?
6. Do you review and rebalance your portfolio at least once a year?
7. Do you have adequate health and life insurance in place?
8. Do you sometimes compare your portfolio with others and feel the urge to copy their choices?

Scoring & Reflection:

- **6–8 Yes answers:** You're on the right track — just stay disciplined and keep reviewing.
- **3–5 Yes answers:** You're aware but vulnerable to danger zones. Time to fix gaps.
- **0–2 Yes answers:** High risk! Your financial strategy needs urgent attention.

Safe Investing Habits Checklist

Use this as your quick guide to stay clear of danger zones:

- **Have a written financial plan** aligned with your goals and risk profile
- **Build an emergency fund** (6–12 months of expenses) before chasing returns
- **Review and rebalance your portfolio** at least once a year

- **Limit riskier bets** (F&O, crypto, trading) to <5% of surplus funds only
- **Stick to one trusted financial advisor** to avoid confusion
- **Get adequate insurance** — life, health, and critical illness
- **Check all investments for regulatory approval** (SEBI, RBI, IRDA, etc.)
- **Avoid comparing portfolios** — focus on your journey, not others.’
- **Never chase guaranteed returns** or “get-rich-quick” schemes
- **Discuss your financial plan with family** so they’re aware and protected

Chapter 27

My Journey — from Fear to Freedom

"Everything you've ever wanted is on the other side of fear."

— George Addair

"Adversity introduces a man to himself." – ***Albert Einstein.***

Early Roots of Values

I was born in a humble yet value-driven Maharashtrian family at Dahanu, a small town near the Maharashtra–Gujarat border. My grandfather, a freedom fighter from Chinchani, was deeply respected as a social worker in our Panchal community. His courage, honesty, and service left an imprint on me very early in life.

My father worked in government service (Tarapur Atomic Power Station), and my entire schooling happened in Kendriya Vidyalaya (Atomic Energy Central School, Tarapur).

Life in the government colony was simple, yet rich with cosmopolitan exposure and community living. We had access to a recreation club, canteen, and huge playgrounds.

Me and my younger sister and I grew up learning the value of money because resources were always limited. My mother supported the family through her tailoring work, and both my parents instilled in us the belief that education was the greatest wealth.

"Education was my father's biggest dream for us. Money was limited, but values were unlimited."

When it was time to choose between a costly engineering degree at a private Engineering College outside of Mumbai or a more affordable B.Sc. in Mumbai, I chose the latter to ease my father's financial burden.

Hostel life at Wilson College taught me resilience and independence. To support my expenses, I took up home tuitions and eventually even a sales job with a Xerox dealer before my graduation results.

I was eager to learn, grow, and become financially independent — even if it meant starting small. Hence, alongside my sales job at a leading Direct Sales Associate (DSA) of **Modi Xerox,** I pursued and completed a part-time Post Graduate Diploma in Marketing and Sales (PGDMS).

The Spark of Finance

The turning point came when I joined Genesis Integrated Services, a DSA for **Bank of America**, and got into the Banking and Financial Services Industry. Suddenly, I was exposed to the world of retail banking, loans, assets, liabilities, and, most importantly, wealthy clients living in South Mumbai.

Watching business owners and stockbrokers leverage their money made me realise one profound truth: most wealth is built and multiplied through equities. Meeting high-profile clients who pledged crores worth of shares opened my eyes to money mindsets and financial leverage. Those were my first lessons in wealth creation—and they stayed with me forever.

"Wealth is built and multiplied not through gold, bank FDs, or real estate but equities."

At only 23, I was entrusted to lead a team of senior sales managers, many of whom were older and more experienced than me. Later, my journey took me through reputed brands like **National Panasonic, ICICI Prudential, Aditya Birla, and Max New York Life,** and each of those brands enriched me with invaluable learnings and experiences.

Professionally, I was climbing fast, earning promotions, recognition, completing my part-time Master's Degree (MHRDM), and even buying homes in Virar and Borivali. Personally, I was improving my lifestyle, building a family with my wife, Harshal, and together we pursued our dream of becoming parents.

But beneath the achievements lay hidden cracks—financial mistakes and emotional struggles that would bring my life to a standstill.

The Fall — A Collapse of Finances, Feelings, and Faith

Between 2003 and 2008, I got addicted to swing trading. Despite generating high short-term returns, I failed to build wealth. I lived beyond my means, juggling two EMIs, indulging in branded consumption, and saving barely 10% of my income.

When the 2008 Lehman crisis hit, the financial services industry collapsed. By June 2009, I lost my job. Around the same time, our first IVF attempt failed, draining us emotionally and financially. To make matters worse, my EMI bounced for the first time — on the very day I attempted my final CFP exam.

"High Income or a rising career is useless without high savings and investing discipline."

The combination of professional failure, financial stress, and personal heartbreak pushed me into severe depression. I suffered panic attacks, rage, and sleepless nights. My wife, Harshal, stood by me like a rock, even as my family rushed in to support, but I had hit rock bottom. At one point, I even resisted psychiatric help, unable to recognise myself.

Those six months were the darkest period of my life. I had lost confidence, cut off from the world, and questioned the very meaning of my existence.

"When everything collapsed— career, money, even dreams of parenthood— I collapsed from within."

The Rise — An Ascent of Clarity, Confidence, and Purpose

And then, light appeared. Harshal introduced me to the Art of Living - Dynamism for Self & Nation (DSN) course. Through Sudarshan Kriya, meditation, and devotion, I released my pent-up emotions and reconnected with myself.

For the first time in months, I slept peacefully. During deep meditation, I had my "aha" moment when I discovered my true purpose: "To help people manage money better, avoid mistakes I had made, and live freely".

"In stillness, I found my life purpose: To guide others from fear to freedom."

We created our own Financial Plan, cleared loans, built an emergency fund, and began investing towards our top priority goals. Slowly, clarity and confidence returned.

I rejoined the corporate world briefly with Tata AIA to stabilise finances, but my mind was set on entrepreneurship.

By November 2011, I launched **Adyanta Financial Services (Adyanta)**, inspired during meditation. The name itself—Adyanta (a combination of 2 Sanskrit words - Aadi and Anta, meaning beginning to end)—symbolised my renewed journey. In May

2013, our son Jairaj was born through our second IVF attempt, bringing joy and luck. That same year, I received my first National Award in Goa.

From there, **Adyanta** grew steadily by collaborating with top brands like TCS, Accenture, and Tata Motors through financial awareness workshops and worksite activities. Over time, these associations turned into loyal clients who fueled our growth through word-of-mouth, enabling us to impact over 1,000 families worldwide.

From Scarcity to Abundance

Our Journey of Dreams — Vipul & Harshal's Bucket List

Looking back, my journey has been one from fear to freedom. Fear of money, of failure, of not being enough—transformed into financial freedom, clarity, and purpose.

Today, I enjoy multiple streams of income, a bucket list actively being ticked off, and the privilege of contributing towards causes close to my heart. Harshal, too, has transitioned from Tata

Consultancy Services to join **Adyanta** full-time (as the Chief Administrative Officer) — turning this into our shared purpose and joint mission.

We both now perfectly complement each other's strengths, pursue our passion, practice gratitude, and live by the mantra: **Live More, Give More.** Because true wealth is not just in what you accumulate, but also in the happiness you share and the lives you touch.

"True wealth is not what you hoard, but what you share."

Key Takeaways:

1. **Money Lessons Start Early**— Childhood values and family circumstances shape our financial habits.
2. **Wealth Needs Strategy, Not Just Income** —Trading or high income without savings and planning creates stress, not freedom.
3. **Crisis is a Turning Point**— Sometimes, losing everything clears the path to your true purpose.
4. **Support Systems Matter**— Family, spouse, mentors, and spiritual practices can lift you when nothing else can.
5. **Financial Freedom = Clarity** — A written plan with goals, priorities, and numbers is the first step towards financial freedom.

6. **Character is the true foundation of wealth** — integrity outweighs money as it's the long-term asset that builds trust.
7. **Freedom Comes with Giving**— When you align money with your passion and purpose, life becomes meaningful.

"From fear to freedom is not a straight path—it is a conscious journey of learning, unlearning, and giving. If I can make it, so can you."

Begin your journey today...

Chapter 28

Recommended Books — My all-time Favourites

"A reader lives a thousand lives before he dies."

— George R.R. Martin

*"The man who does not read good books is no better than the man who can't." — **Mark Twain.***

Beyond my certifications and real-world experience, some of my most valuable lessons came from the pages of these remarkable books.

These are the books that shaped my thinking, challenged my beliefs, and gave me timeless strategies to build wealth and live with purpose.

Each one is a gem—offering perspectives that can help you not just earn more, but live more.

Recommended Books:

1. Rich Dad Poor Dad — Robert T. Kiyosaki

A personal finance classic contrasting the money mindsets of the author's "Rich Dad" and "Poor Dad."

It teaches the importance of financial education, assets over liabilities, and building passive income.

The book inspires readers to think like investors, not just employees.

2. The Millionaire Next Door — Thomas J. Stanley & William D. Danko

Reveals that most millionaires live modestly, save diligently, and invest wisely—not lavishly.

Based on research, it debunks stereotypes of wealth and highlights disciplined habits.

A guide to building wealth quietly, without lifestyle inflation.

3. Your Money or Your Life — Vicki Robin & Joe Dominguez

A life-changing book linking money with personal fulfillment.

Teaches tracking every expense, redefining "enough," and aligning spending with values.

Focuses on achieving financial independence while living a meaningful life.

4. I Will Teach You to Be Rich — Ramit Sethi

A no-nonsense, action-oriented personal finance book for millennials and young earners.

It covers banking, saving, investing, and automation with a sprinkle of humour.

It encourages spending on what you love—while cutting costs mercilessly on what you don't.

5. The Intelligent Investor — Benjamin Graham

The definitive guide to value investing and protecting capital.

Introduces the concept of "Mr Market" and margin of safety.

A timeless manual for long-term, disciplined investors.

6. **Money: Master the Game — Tony Robbins**

This book condenses insights from top financial experts into a 7-step wealth-building blueprint.

It covers asset allocation, index funds, and financial freedom strategies.

Lastly, it motivates readers to take control of their financial destiny.

7. **The Barefoot Investor — Scott Pape**

A simple, practical money management plan using "buckets" for spending, saving, and investing.

It emphasises debt reduction, automation, and stress-free finances.

The book is designed to work for everyday families without financial jargon.

8. **Just Keep Buying — Nick Maggiulli**

This book focuses on the power of consistent investing over time.

Backed by data, it challenges common money myths and prioritises action over perfection.

It encourages building wealth by steadily buying assets, regardless of market noise.

9. **The Simple Path to Wealth — JL Collins**

A straightforward guide to financial independence through low-cost index investing.

It explains why avoiding debt and investing in the stock market is the surest wealth path.

Written in a conversational style, it has an easy-to-apply style.

10. Die With Zero — Bill Perkins

This book challenges the traditional "save everything for retirement" mindset.

It advocates spending intentionally to maximise life experiences before it's too late.

A manifesto for living fully while managing money wisely.

11. The Psychology of Money (2020 Edition)— Morgan Housel

This book explores how emotions, biases, and personal experiences shape financial decisions.

It uses engaging stories to show that behaviour matters more than knowledge in wealth building.

Last but not least, it highlights timeless lessons on patience, humility, and risk management.

12. The Almanack of Naval Ravikant — Eric Jorgenson

A compilation of Naval's wisdom on wealth, happiness, and decision-making.

It covers leverage, lifelong learning, and building a life you don't need a vacation from.

A blend of philosophy, practical advice, and mindset shifts.

Key Learnings:

- Books may not hand you wealth, but they can give you the mindset, clarity, and courage to create it.
- Each book is a mentor in disguise, offering decades of wisdom in a few hundred pages.
- The titles in this list have shaped how I think, decide, and live—and they can do the same for you.
- Let them challenge your beliefs, inspire your actions, and remind you that financial freedom begins not in your bank account, but in your mind.
- The more perspectives you absorb, the stronger your own financial philosophy becomes.

Chapter 29

Glossary — Simplifying Financial Lingos and Jargons

"If you can't explain it simply, you don't understand it well enough."

— Albert Einstein

Decode the most common acronyms and confusing terms in personal finance — made simple for every reader.

"Confused by all the financial jargon? You're not alone — but after this chapter, you'll never be confused again."

Let's simplify the world of acronyms, jargon, and technical terms that make most people switch off.

"Financial literacy is not about jargon — it's about clarity."

Common Acronyms — A Quick Decode

AIF – Alternative Investment Fund

AMC – Asset Management Company

AUM – Assets Under Management

ELSS – Equity Linked Savings Scheme

EMI – Equated Monthly Instalment

EPF – Employees' Provident Fund

ETF – Exchange Traded Fund

F&O – Futures and Options

FD – Fixed Deposit

GST – Goods and Services Tax

IPO – Initial Public Offering

ITR – Income Tax Return

KYC – Know Your Customer

LPCC- Licensed Purpose Coach Certification

NAV – Net Asset Value

NPS – National Pension System

PAN – Permanent Account Number

PMS – Portfolio Management Service

PPF – Public Provident Fund

RBI – Reserve Bank of India

REIT – Real Estate Investment Trust

SEBI – The Securities and Exchange Board of India

SIP – Systematic Investment Plan

STP – Systematic Transfer Plan

SWP – Systematic Withdrawal Plan

TDS – Tax Deducted at Source

ULIP – Unit Linked Insurance Plan

USD – United States Dollar

Technical Terms — Simplified

Asset Allocation – The mix of equity, debt, gold, etc. to balance risk & return.

CAGR – Compounded Annual Growth Rate — how fast your investment has grown annually, on average.

Capital Gains – Profit from selling investments — may be taxable.

Corpus – The total value of your accumulated investments.

Debt – Loans or bonds — lower risk, lower return.

Diversification – Spreading money across assets to reduce risk.

Emergency Fund - 3–6 months of expenses kept liquid for emergencies.

Endowment Plan - Life insurance with savings — low return, high cost.

Equity - Ownership in a business — high growth, high risk.

Index Fund - A mutual fund that mirrors a stock market index like the Nifty 50.

Lifestyle creep - Gradual increase in spending as income rises.

Nominee - The person legally eligible to receive your investments.

Risk Appetite - Your emotional and financial capacity to handle losses.

Step-Up SIP - A SIP that increases annually — helps beat inflation.

Term Plan - A pure life insurance plan with no returns — only protection.

XIRR - Extended Internal Rate of Return — true annual return when cash flows vary.

Financial Jargons — In Plain Simple Terms

InVITs (Infrastructure Investment Trusts) — InVITs are investment vehicles that enable investors to gain exposure to infrastructure assets like highways, pipelines, or power grids. They offer stable cash flows and long-term returns.

Progressive Asset Allocation — An investment approach where your asset mix (equity, debt, gold, etc.) changes gradually over a period of time based on your age, goals, and risk appetite. It's like progressively moving from riskier to safer investments.

REITs (Real Estate Investment Trusts) — REITs allow investors to invest in real estate assets like office buildings and shopping malls without owning them directly. They generate returns via rental income and capital appreciation.

SIFs (Specialised Investment Funds)— With a minimum investment of ₹10 lakhs, SIFs offer a regulated way to diversify beyond traditional investments. They're ideal for high-net-worth investors looking for alternative strategies and specialised portfolios.

Top 5 Takeaways

1. Most financial terms are simpler than they sound.
2. Learn the acronyms you encounter often — they're repeatable.
3. Focus on clarity over complexity — don't chase fancy jargon.
4. Ask your advisor to explain terms — no question is silly.
5. Empowerment begins with understanding — keep learning.

Chapter 30

The 30-Day Action Plan — From Intention to Implementation

"The journey of a thousand miles begins with a single step."

— Lao Tzu

A simple, powerful, step-by-step challenge to take control of your money in just one month

Don't wait for the perfect moment to manage your money. Start with 30 days — and change the rest of your life.

This plan is designed to give you clarity, direction, and momentum. One step a day. Zero overwhelm. Maximum impact.

Week 1: Awareness & Clarity

Day 1: List all your income sources.

Day 2: Track your expenses — use an app or notepad.

Day 3: Categorise spends into needs, goals, EMIs, and lifestyle.

Day 4: Identify 3 wasteful expenses to reduce next month.

Day 5: Write down your top 3 financial goals with timelines.

Day 6: Check all your bank accounts and consolidate if needed.

Day 7: Calculate your net worth (assets - liabilities).

"Clarity is power. Financial clarity is financial freedom."

Week 2: Protection & Preparedness

Day 8: Review your term and health insurance.

Day 9: Add nominee info in all your financial accounts.

Day 10: Check if you have 6 months of expenses as an emergency fund.

Day 11: Start or top up your emergency fund.

Day 12: List down your loans, interest rates & EMIs.

Day 13: Prioritise closing high-interest debts.

Day 14: Discuss financial priorities with your family.

"Protection is wisdom; preparedness is freedom."

Week 3: Planning & Automation

Day 15: Start a SIP for one of your goals (even ₹1,000/month).

Day 16: Set up a Step-up SIP if possible.

Day 17: Create a goal bucket list — education, house, retirement.

Day 18: Tag your investments to each goal.

Day 19: Review and name your mutual funds.

Day 20: Avoid F&O or short-term trading distractions.

Day 21: Automate your SIPs and bill payments.

"It's not about how much you earn. It's about how well you plan."

Week 4: Legacy & Growth

Day 22: Check/update your Will or start writing one.

Day 23: Create a Family Finance Folder (physical + digital).

Day 24: Add logins, insurance, MF, FD, and property documents.

Day 25: Talk to your spouse or kids about your financial plan.

Day 26: Identify your next financial milestone (e.g., 1 Cr corpus).

Day 27: Read or listen to one book or podcast on personal finance.

Day 28: Review your financial coach or advisor relationship.

"Growth builds wealth; legacy gives it meaning."

Final 2 Days: Reflect & Recommit

Day 29: Write down your biggest money learning this month.

Day 30: Set 3 new rules for yourself — and stick to them.

"You're not behind. You're just getting started — and that matters."

Top 5 Takeaways

1. Small steps, done consistently, create financial momentum.
2. 30 days is enough to reset your financial mindset.
3. Awareness precedes planning — track, reflect, act.
4. Automation builds consistency — even without motivation.
5. Your goals deserve attention. Your money deserves a plan.

Chapter 31

10 Money Mantras & The Adyanta Financial Freedom Formula

"Wealth consists not in having great possessions, but in having few wants."

— Epictetus

"Clarity precedes mastery. Simplicity sustains it."

As we conclude this journey, here are the distilled truths — the essential money lessons that matter across income levels, life stages, and market cycles.

1. **Mindset Matters More Than Money**

    - Wealth begins with belief and discipline, not a large pay cheque.
    - A scarcity mindset creates stress, while an abundance mindset builds wealth.
    - Don't chase returns — chase purpose, structure, and progress.

2. **Budgeting Is a Tool for Freedom, Not Sacrifice**

    - A budget gives you control — not restriction.
    - Know your income, track your spending, and automate your savings.
    - Create space for joy without sabotaging your future.

3. **Protection Comes Before Growth**

    - Insurance is not an investment — it is your safety net.
    - Health cover, life cover, and an emergency fund must be in place before you grow wealth.
    - One crisis can wipe out years of progress if you are

unprepared.

4. **Goals Make Money Meaningful**
    - Money without goals leads to random outcomes.
    - Plan for milestones — children's education, a home, retirement, holidays, giving.
    - Investing is simply goal-setting with numbers attached.

5. **Long-Term Investing Beats Short-Term Trading**
    - Time in the market matters more than timing the market.
    - Equity is powerful — if you give it time.
    - Stay invested through ups and downs. Noise is temporary; compounding is permanent.

6. **Asset Allocation and Discipline: Define Returns**
    - Success depends more on asset allocation and discipline than on choosing the "best" fund.
    - Know your time horizon and emotional risk tolerance.
    - Diversify across asset classes — but don't overcomplicate.

7. **Taxes, Reviews, and Rebalancing Are Not Optional**
    - Smart tax planning means more money left to grow.
    - Annual reviews ensure alignment with your goals.
    - Rebalancing is how you "book profits" without trying to predict market tops and bottoms.

8. **Avoid Get-Rich-Quick Traps**
   - Crypto hype, F&O speculation, Ponzi schemes, and shady "gurus" — know what to avoid.
   - Build slowly. Protect fiercely. Grow wisely.
   - 90% of wealth creation is simply avoiding costly mistakes.
9. **Money is a Family Affair**
   - Involve your spouse. Educate your children.
   - Talk about money openly — including inheritance, wills, and family values.
   - Financial literacy passed down is far more valuable than money passed down.
10. **Freedom is the Ultimate Goal**
    - Money is a means — not the end.
    - The goal is not riches; it is choices, security, peace of mind, and purpose.
    - True wealth = Health + Time + Relationships + Financial Independence.

The Adyanta Financial Freedom Formula :

RI + ER + SA + SIP (30%) = Financial Freedom

Where:

RI → Right Insurance (Health cover: 5–6× annual income; Term cover: 15–20× annual income)

ER → Emergency Reserve (3–6 months of monthly outflows)

SA → Smart Allocation across 5 asset classes (Equity, Debt, Real Estate, Gold + Silver, Cash)

SIP(30%) → 30% income discipline via SIP

Disclaimer: This is a general framework and may not apply to everyone—especially individuals aged 50+ or with an annual income above ₹50 lakh.

Protect right.

Prepare early.

Allocate smart.

Commit 30%.

Live Freely.

"Protect first. Allocate right. Commit consistently."

Your Next Step

If this book inspired you to take action, review your finances today:

- List your financial goals.
- Create a Smart Household Budget.
- Review your insurance, investments, and income.
- Speak to a financial advisor or coach if needed.
- Take your first step — even a small one.

Because clarity creates momentum, and momentum creates freedom.

Chapter 32
Financial Freedom Beyond Money

"The greatest wealth is freedom."

— Cicero

You now have the knowledge, the tools, and the mantras to act. But before we close this journey, let's pause and reflect.

Because true financial freedom is not just about money — it's about the life you **create with it.**

"Freedom starts where money ends — when money stops driving your life and starts enabling it."

The True Wealth Equation

When we think of wealth, our minds instinctively turn to numbers — bank balances, investment portfolios, and retirement corpus figures.

But real wealth has always gone far beyond digits on a statement.

In my coaching journey, I've met people with crores in the bank but no peace of mind.

And I've met others with modest means who live joyfully because they understand that.

Money is essential — it fuels choice and enables independence.

But it is only one piece of a much larger puzzle. Without the others, freedom remains incomplete.

The Financial Freedom Equation

Financial Freedom is never just about money. It is the sum of five essentials — Health, Time, Purpose, Relationships, and Money. When these elements work together, they create a life where you're not just financially secure, but mentally grounded, physically strong, deeply connected, and aligned with what truly matters.

Financial Freedom = Health + Time + Purpose + Relationships + Money

Freedom is holistic — and this equation shows you how to build it.

"True wealth isn't money alone - it's time to live, health to enjoy, and loved ones to share it with."

Now, let's dive into the four essentials beyond money:

1. Holistic Health & Wealth — Two Sides of the Same Coin

Health and wealth are inseparable.

One sustains your body; the other sustains your journey.

Without health, wealth loses its joy.

Without financial stability, peace of mind erodes.

True freedom emerges when both are in harmony — when you

nurture your body, mind, and finances with equal intention.

Just as you invest through SIPs for your future, invest in your well-being today — through regular check-ups, mindful movement, spiritual practice, nourishing food, and hobbies that recharge your energy.

"You can't enjoy wealth if you're not in good health."

Client Story: Darshana's Journey to Inner Peace

My sister Darshana, an Innovation Consultant at TCS and once a deeply emotional and introverted soul, was shattered when we lost our mother to cancer a decade ago. The grief ran deep, and healing took years.

But over time, I witnessed a remarkable transformation — a journey from grief to grace.

Through self-awareness, spiritual practices, and inner work, she learnt to find balance within.

Recently, when our father lay on his deathbed, she was not overcome by despair. Instead, she radiated calm gratitude — praying for his peaceful transition and embracing the cycle of life and death with rare serenity.

Today, she lives mindfully — practising yoga, eating consciously, and radiating quiet strength. She has not just achieved financial freedom, but something deeper: **freedom from emotional pain, inner peace, and holistic well-being.**

"Holistic well-being isn't just a fit body — it's a calm mind, a happy heart, and a content soul."

2. Time Wealth — Owning Your Calendar

The most underrated form of wealth is **time.**

Having the freedom to choose how you spend your day is a luxury money alone cannot buy.

Financial independence does not mean quitting work — it means having the freedom to choose what, when, and how you work.

Imagine being able to take Fridays off, begin a passion project, or spend more time with loved ones — without financial stress dictating your choices.

Ask yourself:

"If I had one free day every week, how would I spend it?"

Your answer reveals what you truly value.

Client Story: True Wealth — The Freedom to Be Present

Yogesh Babrekar, MD at Yayanti Exim Pte Ltd, is a global entrepreneur who spends over 150 days a year travelling across continents. Yet despite this pace, he embodies a deeper kind of wealth — the freedom to be fully present.

Our families have shared a bond for three generations, and Yogesh keeps that legacy alive. He shows up for everyone — not just for celebrations, but when it truly counts. When an employee suffered a stroke, he was in the hospital. When his aunt passed away, he cancelled international trips and stayed through all 12 days of family rituals. And no matter where he is in the world, he always returns home for the Ganesh festival.

I've experienced this "true wealth" myself. He attended the inauguration of my first office in 2012 and became my first client. Recently, when my father's health collapsed in the ICU, Yogesh dropped everything and rushed to be with me — staying till midnight, returning for the funeral the next morning, despite heavy rains and being present at the prayer meeting and 13th-day rituals like a younger brother.

That day taught me a powerful truth: real financial freedom isn't about money — it's about the time, presence, and heart to show up for the moments that matter most.

"Being rich is having money; being wealthy is having time."

3. Purpose & Giving Back — The Freedom of Fulfillment

Wealth without purpose can feel hollow. True financial freedom blossoms when you use your resources to serve, uplift, and contribute.

When money becomes a **means to create impact,** life gains depth, direction, and fulfillment.

"Legacy isn't what you leave behind in assets — it's the kindness, values, and light you spread while you're here."

Client Story: Wealth with Purpose

For Adv. Seema Sharma — an engineer-turned-lawyer-true — true freedom came not from earning more, but from serving with meaning.

Her journey began when her brother faced a painful legal battle. Moved by injustice, Seema left her engineering career to study law, dedicating her life to fighting for the underprivileged.

Last year, Destiny revealed her higher calling. A devotee of Swami Samarth inspired her to establish a Swami Samarth Math (temple) in Malavali, near Lonavala. Miraculously, the landowner offered his land for this divine purpose, and within months, hundreds of devotees joined the mission.

Today, Seema practises law, serves society, and heals others through Reiki — merging purpose, service, and spirituality.

Her life is a reminder that freedom feels complete only when wealth serves a higher purpose — to do good, create impact, and give back with gratitude.

"When wealth finds purpose, prosperity turns into peace."

4. Meaningful Relationships — The Freedom of Connection

Financial stress is often the root of family conflict. But when money is managed with openness, it becomes a bridge — strengthening relationships instead of straining them.

Families flourish when **financial planning becomes a shared conversation** rather than a silent burden.

Couples setting goals together, parents teaching children about money, siblings supporting one another — these are acts of love, not just logistics.

"True freedom is found in relationships that let you be yourself — and still inspire you to grow."

Client Story: The Richness of Relationships

At a surprise 50th birthday celebration for my client and friend Rajiv Pandey, Vice President of Technology at Tata Motors Ltd., hosted with great affection by his wife Shweta and daughter Shreya, I witnessed something truly extraordinary.

Among the fifty guests were colleagues, seniors, friends, in-laws, and neighbours — people from across two decades of his life. Each spoke of Rajiv with deep affection and pride, grateful to have shared chapters of his journey.

Their words weren't mere compliments, but living proof of the warmth, humility, and integrity with which he had touched their lives.

Despite the demands of a senior corporate role, Rajiv always makes time for people — a thoughtful message, a quiet gesture, a presence that makes you feel valued.

Under those twinkling lights, I realised something profound: **true freedom isn't found in status or success,** but in the relationships that celebrate who you are long after titles fade.

"True freedom isn't counted in currency, but in the bonds and values that outlast it."

True Financial Freedom

Freedom is balance — between wealth and well-being, ambition and peace, self and others.

Financial freedom is not measured by the **size of your portfolio,** but by **the quality of your life.**

It's the freedom to say no without guilt, to give without fear, and to live without compromise. It's about awareness, alignment, and authenticity.

Financial Freedom isn't just about money – it's about balance.

"True financial freedom is living life on your terms — with joy, peace, and purpose."

A Life That Defines Freedom Beyond Money — The Story of Mr Sanjay Shah

When I think of true freedom — the kind that outgrows money, fame, and success — one name stands tall: **Mr Sanjay Shah,** Founder & MD of **Prudent Corporate Advisory Services Ltd.**

I've known him closely for over a decade, and if there's one thing his life has taught me, it's this:

- He didn't just build a business.
- He built a life rooted in values, purpose, and people.

In 1995, while enjoying a stable, comfortable life in Dubai, he made a choice few would dare:

He returned to India — not for opportunity, but for family.

That one decision set the foundation for everything that followed.

In 2000, he started his entrepreneurial journey from scratch — no legacy, no cushion, no shortcuts. Just clarity, conviction, and relentless action.

And the journey that followed is nothing short of iconic:

- From a one-room office to Prudent House
- From a handful of clients to a presence across 21 states
- From CA to visionary Business Leader
- From a dream to a multi-bagger listed on BSE & NSE.
- From obscurity to building one of India's fastest-growing financial services groups with an AUM of over ₹1 Lakh Crores.

But his greatness isn't in what he built. It's in what he never lost.

Sanjaybhai is the same grounded, warm, people-first person I met years ago. Titles never changed him. Success never owned him.

I still remember our Prudent Loyalty Club - 2014 trip to Bangkok, when Jairaj was very young then. Sanjaybhai lifted him, played with him, and hugged him like family — with pure affection and zero pretence.

That is who he truly is.

And then came the gesture that defines his spirit:

He gifted ₹45 crore worth of his own promoter shares to 650 employees — including the housekeeping staff at his own home.

No cameras. No noise.

Just gratitude.

Just believe that growth must be shared.

His values are his superpower:

- Passion and discipline
- Purpose-driven leadership
- Deep respect for relationships
- Health, humility, and ethics
- Showing up for people — always

Through his vision and actions, he has empowered millions — distributors, employees, families, investors — quietly contributing to nation-building in the truest sense.

To me, he is more than an industry stalwart.

He is a role model, a mentor in spirit, and a living example of what holistic financial freedom looks like.

Because real freedom is not about what you accumulate…

But about how many lives you uplift, and how human you remain through it all.

"Freedom begins when success stops being about you — and starts uplifting others."

The Freedom Test

Simply tick the statements that apply to you.

- Do I own my time?
- Do I sleep peacefully?
- Do my decisions align with my values?
- Do I prioritise people over possessions?
- Am I living my purpose?

How Much is Enough?

A Lesson from the Happiest People I've Met.

Across 25 years of my professional journey, I've interacted with thousands of people — entrepreneurs, CXOs, business families, professionals, and even billionaires. Yet the deepest lessons on wealth, contentment, and what "enough" truly means came from people far outside boardrooms.

Nearly two decades ago, on a trip to Agra and Mathura, Harshal and I met Mahaveer — a cab driver who became our guide, storyteller, and friend over the course of three days.

With no Google Maps or GPS, he crafted our itinerary, narrated the history of every fort and Temple, and took us to hidden eateries and local bazaars based on our tastes.

He spoke openly about his childhood, his family, his finances, and his dreams — with honesty, warmth, and calm acceptance.

When we tried giving him a baksheesh (gift), he gently declined and said:

"Bhagwan ne jitna chahiye, utna de rakha hai… usse zyada ka kya karna?" *meaning "God has given me everything I need. Why chase anything more?"*

His dignity was richer than wealth.

Over the years, I met many more like him:

- Artisans who accept only payment for work, not tips.
- Young couples who left urban comforts to run NGOs in remote villages.
- A juice seller at Worli Sea Face who sells wheatgrass juice for ₹20 and offers neem juice free because *"Neem toh ped se mil jaata hai."*

Different lives. Same essence.

They know exactly how much is enough.

In contrast, I've seen wealthy individuals endlessly accumulate —

often compromising peace, values, and health.

Some chase money until a doctor gives them a deadline.

Some struggle to donate even 2% of what they earn.

The irony:

Those who have far more than they ever need often feel they don't have enough.

Those with very little often live with joy, balance, and gratitude.

True wealth is not measured by accumulation but by awareness — the awareness of what is enough.

"True Wealth begins the moment you stop asking, 'How much more?' and start realising, I already have enough."

Reflection

- What does "enough" mean to you?
- Where in your life are you chasing without clarity?
- What parts of your life already feel abundant?
- If you stopped chasing money blindly, what would you gain?

- Who are the Mahaveers in your life — people who live richly without having much?

"When you know what is enough, everything else becomes a bonus."

Your Turn

List the intangible assets that define freedom.

For instance: sleep in peace, time with family, not checking phones constantly, no debt burden, ability to say "No", doing meaningful work, living with integrity, health of body & mind, connection & joy, or a sense of purpose.

My Intangible Assets that define Freedom:

____

____

____

Now define **financial freedom** in your own words — write a single sentence that captures your vision. Complement it with a visual (optional) that symbolises what freedom looks like for you.

Let it reflect what truly matters.

*Years from now, let that sentence or visual remind you why you worked, saved, invested — and most importantly — **why you lived.***

My Definition of Financial Freedom:

Reflection

Your Journey Begins

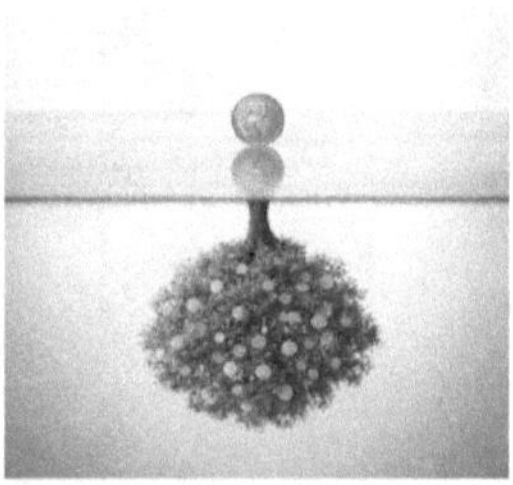

"The secret of getting ahead is getting started."

— Mark Twain

Congratulations!

You've walked through six pillars and thirty-two chapters—more than numbers, a complete framework guiding you toward financial clarity, confidence, and freedom.

- **Mindset & Awareness** — opened doors.
- **Protect & Prepare** — gave strength.
- **Grow & Allocate** — built wealth.
- **Retire & Pass On** — added purpose.
- **Adapt & Evolve** — ensured relevance.
- **Reflect & Apply** — tied it all together.

Just as 32 teeth signal maturity, 32 Brahma Vidyas preserve timeless wisdom, and compounding (2^5) unlocks exponential progress, these 32 chapters are designed to shape you—while the six pillars become the steady foundation you can rely on for life.

Together, they form a **temple of financial freedom**—not for worshipping money, but for the life it enables.

As you reach the end of this book, return to the very first exercise — your Dream Wheel of Life. You began this journey by imagining the life you desire across health, family, career, money, contribution, relationships, passions, and inner peace.

Now, pause and reflect:

What would it take to bring balance to this wheel?

What changes, habits, and decisions will help you move closer to the scores you set for your dream life?

True financial freedom is not just about wealth — it's about alignment. When each area of your wheel moves in harmony, you experience holistic freedom: clarity in your goals, confidence in your path, and calmness in your heart.

Let this moment be your full circle — a gentle reminder that your best life is not a distant destination, but a conscious design crafted through intention, discipline, and balance.

But remember: **knowledge alone doesn't create freedom — action does.**

Take one step **today.** Stay the course. Evolve with time.

True wealth isn't measured by money alone—it's in the **health you preserve, the time you cherish, the relationships you nurture, the happiness you spread, and the legacy you leave.**

This book ends. Your journey begins.

Step forward with courage. Shape your life with intention. Claim your freedom.

Choose boldly. Live fully.

From Knowledge to Freedom

Knowledge shows the way. Action sets you free.

Take a moment to pause.

You've travelled through the pages, stories, lessons, and reflections — each one leading you a step closer to clarity, confidence, and calm.

Now, close your eyes.

Breathe deeply.

Feel gratitude for the journey — for the awareness you've gained, and the freedom you are creating.

And as you gently place your hand on your heart, repeat three times —

with conviction, with faith, and with joy:

"I am happy.

I am healthy.

I am wealthy.

I am free."

Let these words echo within you.

For when belief aligns with action, and purpose meets peace, true freedom begins.

ADYANTA
FINANCIALS
Building Trust. Unlocking Freedom

References & Resources

This unified reference list compiles all sources, studies, frameworks, books, and thought-leadership materials cited across the 32 chapters of your book.

1. Global & National Financial Literacy Sources

- SEBI – Investor Education Resources & Mutual Fund Regulations
- RBI – Financial Literacy Framework, Household Finance, Interest Rate & Debt Market Data
- IRDAI – Annual Reports, Consumer Education & Insurance Guidelines
- AMFI – Mutual Fund Handbook, SIP Studies, Asset Class Education
- NISM – Investor Awareness Modules
- PFRDA – NPS Rules & Withdrawal Guidelines
- EPFO & PPF – Provident Fund Rules & Nomination Guidelines
- Income Tax Department – Official Tax Rules, Capital Gains Guidelines
- CBDT – Circulars & Notifications

- Ministry of Corporate Affairs (MCA) – CSR Rules
- Ministry of Women & Child Development

2. Indian Economic & Market Data Sources

- RBI – Inflation, Savings & Household Consumption Reports
- NSSO – Consumer Expenditure Surveys, Household Savings, Labour & Women's Finance Data
- Economic Survey of India
- NSE/BSE – Market Data, Index History & Volatility Trends
- CRISIL – Mutual Fund Rankings & Performance Research
- Value Research – Fund Analysis & Tools
- Morningstar – Fund Ratings, Rebalancing & Behaviour Gap Research
- World Gold Council – Gold Market Intelligence

3. Behavioural Finance & Mindset Research

- OECD – Global Financial Literacy Studies, Behavioural Bias Reports, Youth Finance
- MIT, Duke University, Chicago Booth – Behavioural Finance & Investor Psychology
- Stanford University – Money Mindset Studies
- Harvard Business Review – Decision-Making & Human Behaviour

- Harvard Adult Development Study – Happiness & Life Satisfaction
- WHO – Mental Health, Lifestyle & Well-being Insights

4. International Economic Organisations

- World Bank – Financial Inclusion, Global Wealth, Life Quality Indicators
- IMF – Global Market Outlook & India Growth Studies
- UN – World Happiness Report & Women-Specific Reports
- UNICEF – Family Communication & Child Development Frameworks
- NASSCOM – Future Skills & Tech Trends

5. Investment, Markets & Future Trends

- SEBI – Market Modernisation & Categorisation
- AMFI – Goal-based Investing & SIP Frameworks
- RBI – Digital Economy & FinTech Reports
- PwC, EY, Deloitte, KPMG – India Wealth, Tax & FinTech Reports
- MSCI & S&P – Global Asset Class Studies

6. NRI / OCI / PIO Investing & Global Finance

- RBI – FEMA Guidelines for NRIs
- SEBI – NRI Investment Rules
- Income Tax Department – DTAA Rules & NRI Taxation
- KPMG, EY, PwC – NRI Tax & Regulatory Guides

- IMF & World Bank – India Growth Outlook
- Morningstar – Global Investment Reports

7. Protection, Insurance & Medical Costs

- IRDAI – Annual Reports & Warnings on Mis-selling
- Swiss Re Institute – Global Insurance Reports
- WHO – Medical Inflation, Health Cost Studies
- NSSO – Hospitalisation & Health Insurance Data

8. Family Finance & Youth Education

- UNICEF – Child Empowerment & Family Communication
- NCERT – Foundational Learning
- OECD – Youth Financial Literacy Reports
- RBI – Household Financial Decisions
- SEBI – Beginner Investor Education for Students
- World Bank – Youth Skill Development

9. Giving, Legacy & Estate Planning

- Ministry of Law & Justice – Indian Succession Act, 1925
- Bar Council of India – Will Drafting Guidelines
- MCA – CSR Rules & India Giving
- NGO Darpan – Verified NGO Database
- Charity Aid Foundation (CAF) – India Giving Reports

10. Books & Essential Readings (Across Chapters)

- The Psychology of Money — Morgan Housel

- Rich Dad Poor Dad — Robert Kiyosaki
- Your Money or Your Life — Vicki Robin
- Atomic Habits — James Clear
- Thinking, Fast & Slow — Daniel Kahneman
- Nudge — Thaler & Sunstein
- The Intelligent Investor — Benjamin Graham
- Common Sense on Mutual Funds — John Bogle
- The Little Book of Common-Sense Investing — John Bogle
- A Random Walk Down Wall Street — Burton Malkiel
- The Simple Path to Wealth — JL Collins
- The Millionaire Next Door — Thomas Stanley & William Danko
- Just Keep Buying — Nick Maggiulli
- I Will Teach You to Be Rich — Ramit Sethi
- Die With Zero — Bill Perkins
- The Almanack of Naval Ravikant — Eric Jorgenson
- The Barefoot Investor — Scott Pape
- Personal Financial Planning in India — Madhu Nair

11. Mindfulness, Mental Wellness & Spirituality

- Art of Living - Mindfulness & Spiritual Growth
- Global Mindfulness & Gratitude Research Studies
- Ancient Indian Texts on Abundance & Purpose

12. Tools, Frameworks & Standards

- Financial Planning Standards Board (FPSB)
- AMFI Calculators & SIP Planning Tools
- SEBI Risk Profiling Framework
- AMFI Riskometer
- Portfolio Rebalancing Studies (Morningstar, CRISIL)

13. General Financial Glossaries

- SEBI – Financial Terminology
- RBI – Banking Glossary
- AMFI – Mutual Fund Terms
- IRDAI – Insurance Glossary
- Investopedia – Global Finance Definitions

www.ingramcontent.com/pod-product-compliance
Lightning Source LLC
Chambersburg PA
CBHW061608180926
51615CB00006B/14
* 9 7 8 9 3 4 9 5 0 9 5 2 8 *